THE RISK IN BELIEVING

Don Talafous, O.S.B.

The Liturgical Press   Collegeville, Minnesota

Cover design: Fred Petters

Nihil obstat: Robert C. Harren, J.C.L., *Censor deputatus.*

Imprimatur: ✠ George H. Speltz, D.D., Bishop of St. Cloud. August 11, 1982.

Library of Congress Cataloging in Publication Data

Talafous, Don, 1926–
    The risk in believing.

    1. Christian life—Catholic authors.   I. Title.
BX2350.2.T32   1982   248.4′82   82-17250
ISBN 0-8146-1280-6 (pbk.)

Contents

Preface

What follows is a collection of efforts at understanding some facets of Christian belief and life. These essays, if that term is not too dignified, are meant to encourage thinking about the meaning of the following of Christ in the context of, largely, Catholic Christianity. But it is also definitely my hope that they will have some appeal for other Christians as well. In manner and style the writing is meant to be non-technical, generally terse, and a bit tart. Some of the pieces are not very terse; others not very tart. None, I hope, are too technical for those who read and think a bit about faith and religion.

As I look over what is assembled here, I realize how much every thought I have is indebted to the reading, study and personal contacts of my life. This lack of originality is also attested to by the numerous quotations beginning the sections. I wish it were possible to give sources for all of them but in the course of collecting the good words of others over the years their origins have become uncertain or simply lost. Many came to me at second hand or orally. It may be worth pointing out that these quotations are purposely not taken from Scripture in order to, possibly, be more arresting to readers than phrases they have heard so often. Some of the quotations reinforce what I say; others are more tangential; some are meant to be humorous or provocative.

Thanks are due to the students of St. John's University, Collegeville, who have stimulated me during some sixteen years as their chaplain, to my family both that of blood and that of Benedict and, finally, to the spirit of John XXIII and the Second Vatican Council. In this twentieth anniversary year of the opening of that great Council, we all have reason to be thankful for the liberating changes it has facilitated within Catholicism and in its relation to other Christians and our world in general.

1

I give particular thanks to Rob Wething who read many of these pieces in their most primitive form and encouraged me by his reactions and to Brenda Lane for her typing. More thanks would risk making the gratitude out of proportion to the volume or depth of what follows.

Don Talafous, O.S.B.
St. John's Abbey
Collegeville, Minnesota

Are We Expecting Anyone?

"Nobody with a good car needs to be justified," Haze murmured.
—Flannery O'Connor

There is nothing more irritating than a Savior when you aren't ready to be saved. —D. Sutten

In the ultimate depths of his being man knows nothing more surely than that his knowledge, that is, what is called knowledge in everyday parlance, is only a small island in a vast sea that has not been traveled.
—Karl Rahner

Too many people, too early in their lives, are certain of too many things.
—Hammerstein

Education is the process of moving from cocksure ignorance to thoughtful uncertainty. —Anonymous

"Patience, people, for the Lord is coming." That refrain formed the theme of the liturgy one Advent Sunday while I was serving as a college chaplain. In trying to bring together Advent, summarized in that line, and the religious situation of young people and myself, more questions than answers arose. I write these essays because I believe I have come to understand somewhat and do believe and love the response given to those questions in Jesus Christ. Yet it seemed to me then and still does that the Advent certainty—the Lord is coming—raises many questions, questions which deserve to be pondered by adult Christians.

To college students in Advent one is drawn to say: Patience, people, exams will be over in a week and a half. Patience, people, vacation is coming. Patience, people, skiing in Colorado is just around the corner. Patience, people, you'll be back to home-cooking, family, and old friends in ten days or so. Patience, people, mistletoe and merrymaking are only a couple of weeks away. But—patience, for the Lord is coming? Are we honestly waiting for the Lord to return? Even to come in some special, mystical, sacramental way in our celebration of Christmas?

"Suddenly there will come the Lord whom you seek," says the prophet. But what do we seek? Are we really concerned to clear a path for him or are we just cutting down Christmas trees? Following John's call (Repent!), do we repent as a preparation for the Lord? And repent of what? Are we *that* conscious of being burdened by sin and needing forgiveness, renewal?

One of Flannery O'Connor's friends wrote to her complaining about a novel by a mutual friend. She said that one of the women in the book flies to religion after her husband rejects her; the other after he dies involves herself in religious works. It seems that it makes faith look like a haven for losers. And, she added, "I am always a bit troubled when people regard faith or religion as chiefly a compensation." O'Connor's response: "Perhaps she is right. On the other hand, some kind of loss is usually necessary to turn the mind toward faith. If you're satisfied with what you've got, you're hardly going to look for anything better" (*The Habit of Being*).

Do prisoners, kidnapped victims of terrorism, and their anxious families know more than we middle-class Americans of what it means to wait in patience for deliverance and freedom? Does deliverance or redemption mean anything to college-age people or to any of us? Does belief in the coming of the Lord or the attendant hope require perhaps prior experience of loss and pain, of being thwarted, frustrated?

Has our life, in general, been too sheltered and protected by loving parents and friends, health, and affluence to prepare us to want deliverance, salvation, a savior? Deliverance from what? And say we would find ourselves someday unprotected by good investments and loving people, what good would a savior like Jesus do anyway? What would we expect of him?

John the Baptist asked his hearers to show sorrow for their unfaithfulness to God by symbolically washing in the Jordan. This repentance, he said, opened them to receive the deliverer, the Messiah. Many Hindus, probably most, still purify themselves daily in a combined bath and baptism. Is all this just something for ancient Jews and remote Hindus, unenlightened people who have not had all the blessings attendant on good hygiene and free enterprise?

Or, are we like the alcoholic who doesn't know that he or she has a problem? Is there anything really wrong? Or, is all this talk about waiting, yearning, longing for someone who will come to deliver us—is all this meaningless for our age? For our culture? Do we really need God? Do we need a savior?

We understand fairly well, especially in the years of early adulthood or late adolescence, that we need conversion to our own truth, to ourselves—we need to get away from being just a copy of someone else or someone else's product—but can we see or understand conversion to God? Are the two conversions related or independent?

Is there anything we really want to be saved from or need to be saved from? Has the experience of pain made us long for the Lord's support and presence? Have our moral failures brought us to discouragement? Or would that be over-dramatizing mere bush-league sins? Have suffering and disappointment made us long for something or someone durable, dependable? What does loneliness mean to us? Have we found loneliness a temporary state, curable once we find the right person? Are we sure that it will be over once that person is found? Or, if we have doubts about the elimination of loneliness, does that necessarily mean we expect anything from the Lord's coming in that regard?

Is there really any hunger or thirst that Christ or God can alleviate or meet for us? If not each of us individually, does the world in general possibly need the healing presence and power of *One Who Is To Come?* Or, can't that be taken care of by better distribution of wealth, better laws, more enlightened people? Are Savior, Messiah, etc., possibly mythological terms for what we might better call progress today?

What are we seeking in work or accomplishment, in drink, in love and friendship, in downhill skiing, in music? Ecstasy? Freedom? Release? True selfhood? Perfect union? Are they it or is any one of them it?

Finally, why do we come to church, to Mass, to Communion? Many of us, whatever the reason, are very faithful. But the questions are as much for me as for you: Why do we come? What do we expect? Why have we continued coming? What are we looking for? What do we seek? What do we want? How does the coming of Christ at Christmas or in Communion help? Or, at the end of time, how would that help? Even though the answer or answers to all these questions are, I believe, to be found in actually *living* Christian life, still the needs of mind and heart cannot be simply ignored.

The essays that follow touch facets of these questions not in any systematic way, it is true, but by circling around and over the whole matter. Limited as these essays are in so many ways, they are the result of one man's effort over some decades to face the meaning of being a Catholic Christian. If they seem fragmentary and not totally filled out, that is because work with college students has necessitated my facing the foundations of faith year after year with new students and has kept me perennially aware of the *questions*. The questions and the so-often "bad news" of our world are always in the background as one tries to present the message, the "good news," of Jesus Christ, the Word of God.

What Do They See in Each Other?

If He would give me a clear sign; if He would just cough! If I could see a burning bush or the seas part or my uncle pick up a check.
—WOODY ALLEN

I have always observed that not only I myself, but also those enviable persons who are able to give reasons for their actions, are never really moved and guided by these reasons. What impels us to act is that we fall in love with something; I own that I am all in favor of such falling in love.
—HERMANN HESSE

(A man named Kaiser consults a Rabbi who is sure of God's existence, though not allowed to pronounce his name.) "You ever see him?" asks Kaiser. "Me? Are you kidding? I'm lucky to get to see my grandchildren." (Kaiser:) "Then how do you know He exists?" (Rabbi:) "How do I know? What kind of question is that? Could I get a suit like this for fourteen dollars if there was no one up there? Here, feel a gabardine—how can you doubt?" —WOODY ALLEN

In the same way that silence can be defended at times only by the noise of words, so the nonrational factors involved in our following of Jesus Christ may need a defense by reason. No matter how else we qualify or explain it, that following of Jesus assumes a unique place for Jesus Christ in one's life and thought. And those who use reason with some regularity, say, in their work or the management of any part of their life, justifiably want to use it in religion, in something so momentous as the orientation of their life. Men and women whose lives and actions are overwhelmingly driven by instinct, emotion, spontaneous reactions, may not understand this same concern. The presumption here is that readers of this type of material—material situated somewhere between *Mad* magazine and Thomas Aquinas—*would be* concerned about the rational in their religion.

7

Illustrations of the cult of unreason in religion and in other matters abound in our society and culture. Nevertheless, that should not prevent us from facing up to the question of reason's possible inadequacies in religion. To do so is not to deny its dignity and place in human life; it is merely to stress that it too is no *absolute.* We do act for "reasons" of fear, fancy, fashion, and foolishness. An exponent in his own life and work of the validity and power of the intellect, the great mathematician and scientist Blaise Pascal made this point notably and repeatedly in his classic *Pensees.* "Reason," he wrote, "is a poor thing indeed if it cannot recognize its own limitations." And possibly only those—like him— who have made the effort to stretch their own reason to its limits have any right to talk about its boundaries.

If, like Pascal, we have been taught to listen to the voice of reason, we will naturally look for some satisfaction for our reason in our com- mitment to Jesus Christ. Many adult Christians, of course, do not in- vestigate sufficiently the rational foundations for belief and trust in Christ. They have not looked seriously at the history and formation of the Gospels or the origins and development of the Christian faith. Such inquiry is not out of the reach of people who can read the *Wall Street Journal* or *Time* and some of this would seem to be a necessary step or phase in the justification of one's faith for a thinking believer. Not to use reason to the same degree on religion as we use it in buying a car or deciding on a school is to assume implicitly that religion is a little less than human. *Some study* of our faith must precede a willingness to see the limitations of that same study. Reason should not be dismissed too easily or cheaply. (A good beginning for an adult Christian who has not stretched the mind to understand the foundations of his or her faith would be the Dutch Catechism—called in its English translation *A New Catechism.* A more recent but also more detailed and slightly more de- manding work—but one accessible to college-educated Christians—is Richard McBrien's *Catholicism.* Finally, Andrew Greeley has written a very attractive and accessible book on the essentials of Christian belief called *The Great Mysteries.)*

We like to believe that things proceed very simply from knowledge to willing to love, and from that to decisive action: once we know what is right, supposedly, we love and inevitably do what is right. That is the pattern that reason would lay out for us. At times we excuse our failures in honesty, kindness, chastity—any area—by referring to our lack of understanding and consequently also of motivation. "If I had really un- derstood it, I would have done this or that." One hopes that such a pro- gression has *some* validity. So if we know that apple strudel or Valium, for example, is dangerous to our health, we will skip the strudel or try to overcome the dependency. But that example itself is probably sufficient evidence for most of us of how limited is the validity of this rational pattern in much of our behavior. Many a drinker, glue-sniffer, or pastry-lover knows the dangers but . . . .

The Gospel of St. John helps move us from the intellectual to other factors involved in believing and following Christ. There we read: "If a man loves me, he will keep my word. . . . He who does not love me does not keep my words" (14:23-24). The phraseology about someone who does this and then that sounds quite logical, but a closer look than we often give to such well-known phrases reveals that John has long left the simply rational order of things. He is not saying that he who *knows* the word and is true to it will love the Lord or that he who knows it and loves it will keep it but that *love* will make one true to the word and love will enable one to live up to the word. Elsewhere he is equally sure of his thought when he insists that action and behavior are ways to truth: "He who does what is true comes to the light" (3:21). *Acting* according to what John presents as truth will bring about comprehension, light. "If you obey my word, you will know the truth" (8:31). Not: if you know the truth, you will obey it. Obedience to the word, i.e., conscientious behavior, leads to understanding, to truth, to insight.

One feels apologetic about stressing this but experience seems to show that we accept this rationally inverted order of things only with difficulty. Knowledge about the life of Christ, clarity about the evidence for the reliability of the Gospels, for instance—neither provides a surety that we will live by it or commit ourselves to it. Reason, love, and action are rarely simply related to each other in that clear order. Within the actual living person, things are never as separate and distinct as the theory would have them. They are a good deal messier and unpredictably scrambled. Above all, in responding to another person, our whole self is involved, not simply one faculty no matter how preeminent. How much we're affected by the shape of the nose, the sound of the voice, maybe even the cut of the clothes. And the object, the end, of Christian commitment has presented itself to us—in the incarnation and the Gospels—precisely as a person.

Almost unthinkingly we repeat, "Love is blind." Yet paradoxically we probably advance more often from love to knowledge than from knowledge to love. Passionate or adolescent love may be blind but in the case of a maturer lover it is love that affords insight, that reveals qualities in the other person invisible to the detached observer. The answer to: "What does he see in her?" is "Without his love, you cannot know." Young lovers experience the truth when they stammeringly try to justify their love to interested parents. Their love likely had its genesis in some vague desire or willingness to surrender kindled by something in the other's manner or appearance. No rational analysis or collection of statistical data will ever duplicate it exactly for others.

Enunciating what was a strong conviction of his whole psychology, William James wrote: "Instinct leads, intelligence does but follow." As often as not, some vague interest, some instinctive love, leads us to knowledge and further love rather than the other way around. Abraham Maslow says somewhere that the man who is going to dedicate his life to the study of ducks had better *love* ducks. And what else explains our choice of a topic to study, a vocation to follow, but an initial interest, a desire, that is unexplainable? This seeming irrationality in everyday human relations and behavior is known to all of us and we should not be surprised to see something analogous in our relation to God or Christ.

Some vague desire, some need, some openness—any of these may be much more instrumental in our faith than any systematic study. All of us know examples of such fortuitousness in ordinary life. A favorite example concerns a friend who was working in a library in Berlin. A man dropped in one day and asked for a particular document which she then got for him. They exchanged a few business-like words. Nevertheless, on the strength of that encounter, the woman told her mother that evening: "Today I met the man I'm going to marry." Within a few years they were married and now, some twenty-five years and six children later, they are still happily married. "To know him is to love him" may fit some situations but just as often "To love him is to know him" works equally well.

Once love has begun, love and knowledge interact and stimulate each other. If that is a vicious circle, many have found it to be also a delightful one. Once again Pascal has said it all: "The heart has reasons of which the mind knows nothing."

If reason can be displaced by love, even more can it be displaced by doing, action, experience. Doing something we cannot rationally justify is often, oddly enough, the key to understanding, knowledge, conviction, love. "Try it, you'll like it" works in a great number of areas. At times it is the only way to insight. Doing, acting, working can lead to knowledge and love as well as stem from them. Many matters make sense or provoke an attraction in us only after being tried. Take beer for instance: the ordinary acne-faced, bubble-gum-chewing, malted-milk-drinking teenager finds beer at first bitter. As we all know, some of them reverse their opinion quickly and totally after a brew or two.

Or, to go from the sudsy to the sublime, how do we learn the truth of something like: "He who loses his life for my sake will find it" (Matt 10:39)? Rationally, it defies what we should expect; lived, it can provide the key to happiness and life itself, as evidenced by hosts of mystics and ordinary believers who have tested the words. Or take the communal ritual of Christians: the Eucharist, the Lord's Supper. Ponder as much as you like. Read all you can. Analyze indefinitely. It remains incomprehensible and strange on that level, accessible only through some regular, persistent experience of it.

The way to a fuller Christian life is by no means simply through more information, better courses in theology, more reading, even more stimulating sermons—though *all this can and should help*. Rather, our surrender to the guidance of the Savior, our actual pursuit of goodness, prove the wisdom of his teaching. This seems to touch the profound philosophical truth that, at bottom, truth, goodness, and beauty are inseparably intertwined and that the genuine search for any one of them entails finding the others as well.

The Old Testament psalm says: "Taste and see how good the Lord is" (Ps 34:8). Ultimately that is the only way to know what being a Christian is. Christ spends very little effort, if any, in trying to appease our reason; rather he points to his life and teaching and says: "Come, follow me"—try it. If being a Christian seems a burden, makes no sense, remains a puzzle, maybe we should start from the opposite end. Instead of just thinking, trying to understand—agonizing, for instance, over a personal God in a world of science—we should try carrying out its teaching, testing it, living it.

A Feast for All Seasons

Many times it would be better if Christians knew less about certain details of the Catholic catechism, but had really grasped the ultimate and decisive questions in a genuine and profound way, questions like God, Jesus Christ, his grace, sin, love, the unity between the love of God and neighbor, and prayer.   —KARL RAHNER

I had already learned that everything I did not understand probably had something to it.   —ERNEST HEMINGWAY

The manner and order in which Catholic belief is expressed should in no way become an obstacle to dialogue with our brethren. It is, of course, essential that the doctrine be clearly presented in its entirety. . . . When comparing doctrines with one another, [Catholic theologians] should remember that in Catholic doctrine there exists an order or "hierarchy" of truths, since they vary in their relation to the foundation of the Christian faith.   —*Decree on Ecumenism No. 11*

Who hasn't commented on the decline of the religious practice of Catholics or on their lack of complete orthodoxy? What is most astounding in some of the commentators, however, is the tendency to equate a basically good development with this assumed disintegration of the faith. For instance, some complain: Theologians and priests who have adopted a "smorgasbord" approach to the Christian faith are responsible for the fact that Christians do not speak with one clear voice and for the fact that they practice their religion in diverse ways. Such critics, the context makes clear, have no problem with Scandinavian eating habits, but are complaining about clergy and theologians picking and choosing among Christian teachings those which they like while discarding the rest.

The imagery has possibilities not envisioned by the writer, possibilities of great validity. There *are* items (if one must objectify matters that much) in the body of Christian belief and practice that are in the nature of an entree while other matters are hors d'oeuvres, side dishes, desserts, or like the chocolate a classy hotel puts on your pillow. To recognize this would seem to be the recovery of some sense of discrimination, not a disintegration.

Faced with the seemingly hostile movements of modern history—the Reformation, the growth of modern science, and the spirit embodied in the French Revolution—the Catholic church tenaciously defended every jot and tittle of its religious practice and belief against any whittling; it was a nervous, militant, and intransigent kind of religion. In the grip of this defensiveness, a great number of doctrines and practices came to be regarded as of equal importance. One hardly distinguished between papal documents on women's dress at worship and the Sermon on the Mount. The obligation to confess one's sins by number and kind and regulations about the use of the trombone at Mass, the fifty-two Sundays and the nine First Fridays: all were matters that a Catholic "had to" believe or accept.

And others could know in advance what you believed by just itemizing the subjects in an encyclopedia entry on Catholicism, all clear and of equal value. Scripture, itself, becomes a catalog of truths of equal importance. A theologian of the Reformation period, St. Robert Bellarmine, typifies the attitude. In the course of the Galileo controversy he went so far as to say: "That man would be just as much a heretic who denied that Abraham had two sons and Jacob twelve, as one who denies the virgin birth of Christ" (Stillman Drake, *Discoveries and Opinions of Galileo* [New York: Doubleday Anchor Books, 1957] 163). All were to be equally believed. Up to the Second Vatican Council pastors and teachers seem not to have worried about degrees of importance in directives from Rome; at least they were usually presented with little nuance. Clearly, in practice, no group, not even the Church in her worst days, could act consistently with such a wooden principle. As someone has pointed out, women of fundamentalist persuasion don't generally cover their heads in church and the Vatican has never felt bound by Paul's remarks that a bishop should be a man of one wife. All along there have been exceptions: literate Christians who distinguished essential and vital matters from the trivial, the unknowable, the peripheral.

Catholic involvement in the ecumenical movement, finally blessed at the Second Vatican Council and by the spirit of John XXIII, has forced us to see our practices and beliefs in better perspective if only through observing the religion of other Christians of genuine faith and conviction. Both Catholics and Protestants have benefited by measuring each other's traditions alongside each other. How much does Catholic recovery of belief in the Mass as a banquet, a dinner shared by friends, owe to Protestant preservation of this emphasis? And Protestants are gainers too from Catholic insistence on sacramental signs in the face of opposition from those who would see value only in one man's thundering sermon or the effect of an emotional hymn.

We need to be more aware for our own spiritual life that not every element, every practice or teaching, of Christianity is going to be of equal significance to me personally, for my life and growth, at any one particular moment. To say this is but to recognize a well-known truth of psychology. But it needs saying against the background of the traditional detachment of Christian believing—at least in its orthodox Catholic form—from any influence by individual, personal factors. We have too often forgotten that the truths of Christian living were born in the experience of living according to the way of Jesus Christ; they were more like a driving manual than an explanation of the principles of the auto. The value of the teaching and example of the Savior is validated not simply or primarily by analysis but by being lived.

Elements of the Christian message may wait on experience and circumstances for their relevance in our lives. A line, for example, like "Without me you can do nothing" (John 15:5), may not mean much to a young person alive with confidence and exuberance in the use of talents and powers; he or she may not have encountered the rock-like resistance of reality to one's ideal. To another the words may well express a central, joyous and liberating element in that person's faith: "I am not alone; I am not expected to control every element of my life or environment." We cannot simply ignore factors such as age, the kinds of experience we have had, our circumstances, our needs, even our moods, in our appropriation of the Christian faith. It may be premature to push "Without me . . ." on others or ourselves; human nature may need to feel its own limitations first.

Or take a practice like praying the Rosary, only a few years ago presented to many Catholics by the Fatima devotees as on a par with Sunday Mass and yearly Communion. To some it typifies tedium, to others tranquility. Or the whole central matter of the suffering and death of Jesus: how much can that mean to us if, because of tender years, sheltered life, or happy lot, we have not brushed against anything more harrowing than an upset stomach? While our situation, our age, our feelings, our needs and purposes are not the sole determinants of what is important, still for each of us they are unavoidable factors in appreciating ideas, beliefs, and practices that are presented to us. Too often the Catholic faith has been presented as if these factors were immaterial. We were made to feel equally guilty whether we failed to appreciate the immaculate conception or the resurrection.

William James, that expansive-minded and sane observer of religious experience, concluded that there were of necessity as many religions as there were individuals. In one sense, of course, that is too idealistic: many of us have never thought enough about the subject to have our conclusions termed a religion. To others the comment may appear as an unacceptable simplification, an excessive concentration on the individual and the subjective which ignores what we have in common with so many others. But I think he must be understood, however one-sided his thought, as simply affirming the necessity for personal assimilation of beliefs.

Our individual comprehension and assimilation of the content of our religion is never perfect; it is always at some stage of development. To deny this often means to take a simple dictionary understanding of what words like redemption, Eucharist, and grace mean and assume that they have become part of us, that we have incorporated them into our developed outlook on the world and life. The honest affirmation of a faith with clear limitations—accepting that a particular element of belief means nothing to me—is something we have been reluctant to do in Catholic practice. A serious effort to bring together faith and life should more often lead to something like this testimony of Tolstoy in his diary, written at the age of twenty-four: "I believe in the one, incomprehensible, and good God, in the immortality of the soul, and in the eternal reward of our deeds; I do not understand the mysteries of the trinity and the birth of the Son of God, but I honor and do not reject the faith of my fathers." What James insists on—and this essay also— and what Tolstoy illustrates is that ripeness is, if not all, at least a great part of the reality of our faith. An element in Christ's life, a traditional doctrine of the Christian church, a hallowed practice of the same: each, however valuable in itself, must meet some need, experience, test in our lives before it can really be "mine."

All this is not to deny the core of Christian faith as expressed in the Gospels or creeds but simply to claim, as the Second Vatican Council itself confirmed, that there is a ranking in significance of the elements of the Christian faith. Much remains to be articulated regarding that. In themselves, elements of Christian belief may be less or more important; for us individually their importance hinges on developments in our life, needs of the moment, and the continuing evolution of our character and personality. Our capacity for truth, reality, is—it should be too obvious to stress—limited and conditioned. Similarly, we require time and experience in order to absorb what we can of the Gospel, of Christian tradition.

Does all this mean we are to sit passively on the sidelines and wait for the Christian message to hit us? To leave that impression would be implicitly to deny the necessity of our active involvement, our effort, in unfolding the riches of belief in our life. Throughout the Gospel stories Christ responds or reveals himself insofar as the other party shows some basic openness, some receptivity. He enters Zacchaeus' house in response to Zacchaeus' gesture of interest in him. Each of us must get out on some similar limb to indicate our desire for meaning and life.

To leave the impression that our faith consists solely of what we want to believe or practice would be much too minimal. What we think we need or want or makes sense to us at any particular moment can all be within a very narrow, small, arbitrary spectrum. Think of the danger for both the individual and society when college students choose a course of study solely in terms of what seems likely to help them "make money." Somehow we must make provision for remaining open to matters that we do not here and now understand or appreciate, matters that in a sense lie behind us—the beliefs and convictions of Christians before us—and matters that lie ahead of us—convictions that wait for the right moment to blossom within us. All this is material for another essay: let a few remarks suffice here. In all of life we witness an interaction between what we think, feel, and need and the information, ideas, and practices that are suggested to us or come to us from this person, this book, this speaker, this experience. The strangest and most uncongenial-sounding elements of the teaching of Jesus can find in us, if we remain open, their moment when they express exactly what time has brought us to understand, when they articulate a new awareness within ourselves. Our concern must be to avoid any premature sealing off of our minds and hearts and, ideally, premature will mean not only at eighteen or twenty-five or thirty-five but at any time.

The word that describes our faith—catholic—means all-embracing, universal. If we may go back to that smorgasbord for a moment, a "catholic" taste may include in its appreciation everything from pickled herring to lingonberry pie. While accepting the need for a certain ripeness relative to the whole content of Christianity, we must aim at being more catholic, more responsive to all that God, the Gospel, the universe, our fellow humans, and our experience have to say to or teach us. Our changing life—at one moment content and relaxed, at another anguished and tense, now joyful, now worried—can help us grow toward the fullness of Catholic faith. It will do this if at these varied moments we turn again and again in an open and prayerful way to the gospel, to a reconsideration of the faith that has, so often, been handed down to us.

A Way Through, Not a Way Out

Anxiety is inevitable in an age of crisis like ours. Don't make it worse by deceiving yourself and acting as if you were immune to all inner trepidation. God does not ask you not to feel anxious but to trust in him no matter how you feel.   —THOMAS MERTON

(Encouraging his followers at Jonestown to drink the poison:) It's hard only at first. Living is much, much more difficult.   —REV. JIM JONES

Too often, people have felt Christianity was a miracle drug to make life miraculously easy without suffering and pain. The purpose of Christianity is not to avoid difficulty, but to produce a character adequate to meet it when it comes. It does not make life easy; rather it tries to make us great enough for life. It does not give us escape from life's burdens, but strength for meeting them when they come.   —J. CHRISTENSEN

The great American vice, utilitarianism: everything has to pay, produce results, immediate visible results including God: produce or shut up! That's why so many people are more interested in getting his help in "miraculously" passing a test or meeting a girl or losing weight than in asking for the kind of character which would be able to work with perseverance, be unselfish enough to attract a girl or have enough self-control to pass up the chocolate cake.   —ANONYMOUS

To those who want salvation cheap, and most men do, there is very little comfort to be had out of the great teachers.   —WALTER LIPPMANN

"Why should I shave when I can't think of a reason for living?" (attributed to an authority with the self-effacing name of Jack Smith). As if in answer to that question and in comparably down-to-earth terms, Frederick Buechner writes: "Faith is what gets you out of bed in the morning" —and we could add: helps you make the coffee, brush your teeth, put on a clean shirt. If these present no problem, the moment of truth may

18

come later when we ask: why eat? why go to the office? why greet any-one? why attend another meeting? why be careful about the traffic? In some mental cases, of course, we do see an inability to handle such ele-mentary situations, a kind of failure of nerve. At some time most of us, I imagine, even the apparently sane and physically vibrant, are attacked by some hesitancy about these matters, some weakness in the knees. A bad cold, a little depression, a failure can do it. Whatever else it is in its higher reaches, faith is, on the elemental and practical level, an atti-tude, a conviction, that assures us it's worth getting up in the morning, worth carrying out the demands of daily life.

Needless to say, in the case of the unquestioned life the demand for any kind of faith may not be all that obvious. We *do* seem capable of moving and living quite well for greater or lesser periods of time simply on the power of some instinctual concern for our hide. Varying with the individual, a new restaurant, a shopping spree, or a high-speed ride can fortify our sense of well-being, of being alive. It's only when the tedium and circular nature of Monday, Tuesday, Wednesday, Thursday, etc., gets to us that we feel the need of a justification for it all or recognize with Albert Camus "that there is but one truly serious philosophical [we might say, human] problem, and that is suicide. Judging whether life is or is not worth living amounts to answering the fundamental question of philosophy [we could say, of life]" (*The Myth of Sisyphus* [New York: Vintage Books, 1960] 3).

But, though such moments or days may come, we can still balk at facing basic questions about whether life is or is not worth living. We may try, instead, to fortify failing instincts with a more conscious bravado. In the following excerpt from an interview with a woman of forty who had her days in the television of the early seventies is illustrated a battle between declining vigor and the will to put up a good front. It seems close to what most of us would call despair:

> At forty, without a husband, you realize you only have a few years left when you are vital and able to take care of yourself. . . . I'm scared of old age; all of us are; it's very frightening to be on your own. But it's very challenging. Your body goes to pieces, you get arthritis or cancer, or your liver is going to go to hell. Everything's just going down the tubes. And you're not mar-ried anymore; you're alone. But you hope, when it comes for you, you have some money to pay the doctors and nurses. You hope when it's over, you've had the guts to do your number. . . . that's all there is. You only have your-self to fall back on. I enjoy life immensely. When you hit my time of life, you have to grit your teeth and say, "To hell with it, here I come." But sometimes in the dead of night, it's so very hard. You're alone, and you get scared, and, God, it would help to have somebody to throw an arm

around. A warm body, yeah, that would help. Still, you know, you have to fight it yourself.

"It's very frightening." "But it's very challenging." "You only have yourself to fall back on." "I enjoy life immensely." Give or take a few years, a few changes in our situation, and that might be any of us—desperate, close to an overdose at the bed and an overdraft at the bank. Trying to believe and telling ourselves, against the evidence, that everything we need is at the beck and call of whatever bluster we can muster.

"The warm body" she speaks of may sound a bit minimal in its anonymity, but the context contains an implicit plea for much more. To give adequate importance to faith does not require that we downgrade that love which the woman sees as part of the solution. Yet here, too, she is perceptive enough to see the limitations. "Still, you know you have to fight it yourself" is close to classic statements that, no matter how many friends and loves we might have, we all suffer alone, we all die alone.

Most who are reading this, it can be presumed, are believers in some sense of the word. Equally, many of us just do not see our faith as capable of giving us sufficient enthusiasm and courage to live in its light through all of life's difficult moments even if we are not driven to think of suicide. And, if we do see faith as an all-round antidote to despair, to lack of nerve, to simple boredom, or as the source of our courage and perseverance, we should not endanger it by illusions. Faith will *not* guarantee uninterrupted painlessness or absolute joy. Such a presumption would be unrealistic, contrary to New Testament teaching. Faith can and must grow but never with the un-Christian expectation that after a certain level we will be immune to unhappiness and suffering. How can people talk that way when Jesus, the model of faith and of our relation to God, suffered misunderstanding, hatred, crucifixion, and an untimely death?

What our faith, our trust in Jesus Christ and his Gospel can do, it seems to me, is this: (1) enable us to live, i.e., motivate us for persevering and energetic living; and (2) save us. That is, faith strengthens our adhesion to and trust in Jesus Christ, who has gone through all the events of our life, passed through the worst—suffering and death—to resurrection and eternal life. Joined to him by baptism and faith, we share his relation to the Father and the ability, through him, to ultimately overcome the evils of our life.

But before all this becomes plausible we often need to grow very much in our faith. Our faith needs vigor and central convictions, the latter partly an intellectual matter. It needs some certainties, and these deeply founded. A telescoped model of the necessary growth, a paradigm of the believer, is put before us in that intriguing story of the blind man in chapter 9 of St. John's Gospel. (A complete retelling is no good; read it.) As the blind man is questioned by his hostile interrogators he progresses by degrees to a fuller understanding of and faith in who Jesus is.

In verse 11, after being questioned, he says he was cured by "the *man* called Jesus." In verse 17, in answer to "What do you say about him?" he replies that he is a *prophet*. When his prosecutors raise the objection that they don't know where this Jesus comes from, he answers that *he must come from God* (v. 33). In verses 35 to 38 the blind man confesses belief in the *Son of Man* and calls him *Lord*, titles reserved in John's Gospel for the eternal Son of God and Savior of his people. The man's faith in and understanding of Jesus have moved from the necessary belief that he shared our condition to trust that he is the loving Lord of the universe and his people's salvation, from the conviction that Jesus was human enough to have had "diaper rash as an infant" (Martin Marty's phrase) to the full Christian belief that he is also the unique Son of God in whom we can put our final trust.

That we instinctively look for and require persons and institutions that we can depend upon has been grotesquely dramatized in recent years in such phenomena as Jonestown and a huge assortment of groups cashing in on this need. True religion, most would agree, should leave room for human freedom and risk. But no religion and none of its representatives are automatically free of the temptation to try to be more to people than they should be. And in the incipient believer the correlative tendency is often found: we can be so hungry for certitude and support that we put our trust in any number of only relatively valuable enterprises and people. We put our trust in the free enterprise system, in a group of friends made in high school or college, in a neatly packaged moral system, in a slick promise of peace of mind. We put our trust in music, business, science, a career, achievements, and, most often and above all, in that one person with whom we hope and believe we can grow and live in lasting love, who will always be there.

In most lives a combination of several of these serves as support for us. All have some value, especially the last, another person or persons. And all are open to loss and destruction through failure, change, accident, disease, and death. Mental breakdowns, poor health, depression, changed attitudes, and new interests all show us that persons and achievements and elements outside ourselves can fade or be dissolved. Our need for them tells us also that we are not our own footing.

It is no simple matter of saying that all human and earthly consolations are so much refuse and, because of their shortlivedness, unworthy

of our devotion. We should, therefore, simply put all our trust and confidence in Jesus and find ourselves overwhelmed with joy, peace, and
tranquility. Possibly—just possibly—some few mystics have found the
solution to life's problems in such absolutes, but generally we do not
have the option of resigning from the universe and instantly finding
ourselves in constant and beatific union with God. Transcendental Meditation and similar groups have promised that adhesion to their program
will end all pain and evil and, in effect, take one out of this existence
insofar as it is imperfect, full of risk, and open to pain. But if there is
one great and universal lesson to be drawn from the incarnation of the
Son of God, it is that his way is not a *way out* of the conditions of human
existence but a *way through* them which leaves them basically intact.
Unlike the devotees of flashier faiths, the follower of Christ asks to be
saved from the contamination of evil, not to be delivered from the world
or matter or the human condition. Karl Rahner's statement of the core
of Christian belief puts it beautifully and realistically:

> Jesus Christ, faith and love, entrusting oneself to the darkness of exist-
> ence and into the incomprehensibility of God in trust and in the company
> of Jesus Christ, the crucified and risen one, these are the central realities
> for a Christian.
>
> *Foundations of Christian Faith*, 324.

Faith in Jesus means belief that he truly lived our life, went through
genuine and awful suffering, died horribly, and rose again. Joined to
him, the difficult circumstances of human life are transformed by the
fact that as we go through them *he is with us* (or, we are in him—different ways of stating the basic point). Just as Jesus did not cure every
sick person in the Palestine of his time—he was not out to render phy-
sicians and human care obsolete—neither does he in exchange for faith
remove us from the ordinary challenges, uncertainties, and worries of
human life. He transforms them, puts them in *the* meaningful context
and points to the goal beyond them. Faith consists in our trust that he
is with us and can transform life; it tells us that if we test our belief by
living it, we can come to the adult decision that this is indeed how life
should be lived. The living, the testing, will tell us that, in a very profound way, it fulfills, not that it necessarily thrills.

To expect some imperturbable euphoria to follow from belief in
Jesus is to expect more for ourselves or something different for ourselves than what, for example, his mother received. In the New Testament and in early Christianity she is depicted as the model disciple.
Much contemporary scriptural scholarship confirms also the conviction
that she was, as recent Catholic piety had it, the "mother of sorrows,"

that she did not sit quietly through all the vicissitudes of her Son's life secretly comforted by the sure knowledge that he would come out of every difficulty unscathed. She worried about his "behavior" and she sorrowed over his suffering and death.

Jesus' own promises, as presented to us in the words of the Gospels, contain references to the cross and the necessity of routine day-by-day faithfulness and obedience, e.g., "If anyone loves me, he will keep my words" (John 14:15). Indeed, he does say: "If anyone loves me, my Father will come to him and we will make our dwelling with him" (John 14:23). But not: "If anyone loves me, he will experience untold and constant bliss." Certainly some joy, even some great joy, may be generated as a by-product of our faith. We should be thankful for such occasions but regard them as grace, not something to be presumed any more than we open the morning paper expecting to read all sorts of evidence for humankind's essential lovableness. With growth in faith we should expect some abiding trust to sustain our lives like a deep and relentless bass tone undergirding the often erratic melody of our life.

Woody Allen, that explorer on the edges of serious thought about life and death, is quoted somewhere as saying: "There's no religious feeling that can make any thinking person happy." Granted the dogmatism apparent in such a sweeping statement, it is, in a sense, what I've been trying to say. But Allen's phrasing implies that he is, like so many of us, under the misapprehension that happiness in an empirical and this-worldly sense should be the end-product of religious belief. Too many pop religious books entitled *Jesus, the Way to Joyous Living*, etc., have taken their toll. "No religious feeling can make a thinking person happy," but belief in Jesus (which is not simply feeling, though composed partly of that) does give us a great hope, does help us get out of bed, put on our clothes, eat, and realize that efforts to alleviate suffering are worth making. It does tell us that even if the universe is expanding infinitely—a cosmological theory which brought all activity to a standstill in the youthful and precocious Allen, according to one of his films— there is still a point to our human life, independent of any theory of cosmology.

Faith tells us that human life can be lived with dignity and meaning. Or we can say in response to remarks like Allen's: happiness, no; salvation, yes. All we've been talking about is really what we mean by salvation: a way to live this life with purpose, dignity, and honesty, assured that the struggle and effort are all part of ultimate victory.

C. S. Lewis addressed the same problem with his usual perceptiveness and quiet wit in an essay printed in *God in the Dock*. Asked the same

old question in a slightly different form—"Which of the religions of
the world gives to its followers the greatest happiness"? Lewis responded:

> While it lasts the religion of worshipping oneself is the best. I have an
> elderly acquaintance of about eighty, who has lived a life of unbroken self-
> ishness and self-admiration from the earliest years and is, more or less,
> I regret to say, one of the happiest men I know. From the moral point of
> view it is very difficult! I am not approaching the question from that angle.
> As you perhaps know, I haven't always been a Christian. I didn't go to
> religion to make me happy. I always knew a bottle of port would do that.
> If you want a religion to make you feel more comfortable, I certainly don't
> recommend Christianity. I am certain there must be a patent American
> article on the market which will suit you far better.
>
> Walter Hooper, ed. (Grand Rapids: Eerdmans, 1970) 58–59.

Despite its topicality, that was said some forty years ago. The only amendment we might make would be to say that while America remains fertile
ground for religions that promise to make one happy, many of them
are imported from the Orient.

Founding and Preserving Faith

If, then, faith in Jesus Christ does not guarantee us constant elation, an
enduring "high," thereby "proving" its worth and encouraging us in
its practice, what, then, will help to fortify and preserve this faith? And,
further, how do we move from a limited and elementary faith to a more
complete kind? To trust that our world is in the hands of a God who
loves us with a love that cannot fail, who is always there: to commit our-
self to such a faith cannot be simply a matter of wishful thinking. Too
many experiences militate against an easy acceptance of "God loves
me." If we are to believe that God truly does love us and save us, how
is that faith to be justified?

Jesus Christ must become more for us than some figure like Plato
or Henry Ford; his word must be more to us than any word of Khalil
Gibran or John Denver. But to know him as the Savior who is there in
the dead of night or the heat of day, no matter where we have been, to
know, believe, trust this—how does this come about or become con-
vincingly real?

Ordinarily, it will be of little help to be told that God must give this
grace, true as that is. That is somewhat like being told to go out and inherit
a million dollars. The truth that faith is a gift cannot, of course, be under-
estimated. And the reader I am presupposing undoubtedly feels he or
she has received that gift in some measure—if we use somewhat mate-
rialistic terms. Some receptivity on our part, being open to what is beyond

and other than ourselves, must be there for faith to commence and to grow. As is indicated elsewhere in these pages, that is undoubtedly the most elemental prerequisite on our part, the only preparation we can make, itself a gift, for the grace of faith. But, more actively, what can we *do* once faith is initiated?

What activity on our part can help give this faith a suitable nurture, the right formula for growth? A little reflection will, I think, persuade most of us that it must, first of all, be practiced. (This seemingly inverted logic was treated in an earlier essay.) We must allow its demands to influence the way we live. The teaching of the Sermon on the Mount, for instance, to take a fairly obvious example, by helping to soften the harshness of ordinary human society, demonstrates the wisdom of the teaching and example of Jesus. Adhesion to the priorities of the Gospel can save us from participation in some of the mad pursuits of our culture, world, milieu, and, in the process, show us how truly Jesus Christ is the way through the jungle, the truth about living and the life amid death and decay.

Beyond living the truth, there is prayer and reflection, two matters which easily merge in practice. C. S. Lewis calls it "training the habit of faith" and says that the content of one's belief must be kept before the mind regularly. We do this by reflective reading, prayer, participation in the church's liturgy. Without such persistent attention our belief or any belief, for that matter, will not endure. We speak so often of people losing their faith but no one really loses it in the sense that almost inadvertently we discover it is no longer alive. We kill it, perhaps, or starve it or neglect it and so it may fade away. But since we are responsible for some voluntary and human acts to sustain it, it is much more correct to say that we throw it away rather than lose it.

Prayer and reflection. After the basic attitude of receptivity, of awareness of need and insufficiency, along with the effort to test faith by living it, there must be these two "activities," prayer and thinking. Praying is, for our relation to God, what conversation, a few words, a letter, or a phone call is in any human relationship. Without something of that nature, friends fade out of our lives, are forgotten. For most of us a daily few moments, speaking directly to God, to Christ, about our life and its circumstances and daily content of joys and difficulties makes the relationship real, acknowledges the presence and reality of God. Liturgy (worship) does the same thing in a more formalized and communal way. Even if our conversation, our praying, starts out as almost a sort of talking to ourselves about our life, it can easily slip into speaking to God about it and asking his help, guidance, strength. We will grow in our faith to the point where it gets us out of bed with some zest and through the day only if we consciously practice it by at least adverting through prayer to the one in whom we believe. Faith understandably roots itself in thinking beings only if they consciously reflect on it, give it some time and place comparable to what they spend on gardening, money-making, perfecting their golf game.

As Lewis wrote, faith is not really lost. It slips away or we throw it away by indifference, lack of attention and care. It is not simply a matter of time, obviously, but we must ask ourselves how we expect it to live when the amount of time and attention we give it is so minimal in comparison with the attention we give to television, the daily paper, balancing our checkbook, the care of our skin or hair, our professional and personal ambitions, etc. Faith is a gift that we must believe God is ready to give to anyone. But on the human side it is like the gifts we speak of in human nature—a gift for music, for instance. Without some education and practice, the gift can remain for all practical purposes unborn. Lord, through your gift, I believe; now, help my unbelief (cf. Mark 9:24).

Plainly, this essay has amounted to a restatement of the conviction, developed elsewhere in these pages, that the only proof of faith is in the doing and the participation, that some serenity and confidence come only through prayer and doing the word we have received and thought about. We have been saying also that there is no proxy way to faith or towards building it up. Apart from *our* receptivity and *our* effort, no one else or anything else is going to provide it for us. While faith is not our creation, it will not survive without our nurture.

The Ear and Mouth Relationship

The responsible man is he who tries to make his whole life an answer to the question or call of God.   —D. BONHOEFFER

One must become as humble as the dust before he can discover truth.
—MAHATMA GANDHI

We don't invent God; He reveals Himself. We don't give ourselves to Him; He's the one who gives Himself. All He asks is that we receive Him. . . . Religion consists in what God does for us—those stupendous things He dreams up for us.   —L. EVELY

What faith tells us about our prayer is this: when we pray, we make ourselves receptive to the activity of the risen Lord in creation.
—*A New Catechism*

Whenever we are subjected to the bloated bombast of a political campaign or the hype of advertising there is the temptation to question, at least momentarily, the value of hearing well and the usefulness of speech. But of course, despite all that devaluation and distortion, hearing and speaking are at the heart of our life, intimately related to its meaning. We have ears to hear that meaning, a tongue to tell it.

As we should expect, Christ's words and works in the Gospels are concerned with just such basic elements of human life: health, eating, hearing, seeing, speaking. By describing Christ's miracles of healing in language taken from Scriptures written several hundred years earlier, the evangelists of the New Testament mean to tell us that this Jesus is truly the one expected for so long, the one who will make the blind see, the deaf hear, the mute speak, and the lame walk.

But what do we do today with that message? Do we applaud ourselves because *we* believe that he is the expected one? That we hear so well? Or do we lament that *our* faith seems to merit so few miracles, that so many cancer cases are not cured by prayer or faith? There is more that is expected of us.

First, Christ did not miraculously cure all the afflicted of his day. He did not intend, apparently, to make irrelevant the Mayo Clinic, our doctor, or human kindness. His cures announced that the expected one had arrived, but the cure of the rest of the handicapped and hurting of his time and ours was very much left up to other human beings. Healing is up to us: to our prayer, our medicine and science, the therapy of our daily kindness and concern, our visit to the hospital.

And, further, we need to realize that the boundary between those who cannot hear, those who cannot speak well—on the one hand—and the rest of us who think we hear and speak correctly is *not* all that sharply defined. We all need to be healed; in academic terms, none of us rates a perfect 4.0 for our hearing and speaking. The power of Christ to cure would certainly not have its effect if we were to limit it to the supposed and, to us, obvious afflictions of others. In a very profound sense we all need hearing aids; we all need speech therapy.

With better hearing we would become more attentive to God, the world, our conscience, other people, their needs and suffering, events, history, new situations—all of which speak to us. Too often and too early in life we are tempted to insulate ourselves against any new idea or outlook by leaving our receiver off the hook. All of us would benefit from cleaner hearing, from not merely hearing what we want to hear but what is being said. Very similar points could be made about our seeing, but that is another matter.

To learn to be present to what we are hearing is an exertion for all of us. It would be embarrassing for many of us, for instance, to discover where our thoughts are during a sermon or even during ordinary conversation: probably off water-skiing, anticipating a football game, or remembering an appointment. Hearing is not at all the passive function we so often assume it is. Rather it is an intense and demanding task. To be willing to really hear entails recognizing what we do not know or at least *that* we do not know all we should and entertaining the possibility that we know some things wrongly. It involves a kind of essential humility. An odd verse from Scripture, a criticism from a friend or foe, an idea that challenges our ordinary habits, a bit of uncomfortable and disconcerting news on television or in the paper—any of these, allowed to enter and germinate, can teach us. As in the physical sciences, it is often some troublesome, stubborn happening or fact that causes reexamination and new insight.

Hearing well in turn helps us perceive meaning, produces sense within us; what God, the world, and others have to say to us interacts with what is there already—to help form our personalities and characters. Then, in our speech, we express what we have learned and become. In it and by it we help define ourselves and we help others to hear. Someone has pointed out that we might find in the fact that we have two ears and one mouth some indication of the relative importance of our hearing and speaking. If speaking is to serve its function of expressing meaning, it presupposes some patient hearing. With speech we become involved in convictions, decisions, even promises like one to live with someone for the rest of one's life. With speech we disclose a judgment and run the risk of the consequences. Words once spoken or written are hard to retrieve. But with all their risk and their inadequacy at times in expressing our experience—we need words even to express the inadequacy of words—words do link us with the human family on a most elevated level, that of meaning. All the more important, therefore, is the antecedent hearing, the listening that makes our speech worthwhile.

It is difficult to think of anything more basic and essential to our growth as human beings and Christians than learning to listen and then to speak. Even though we may never regard ourselves as contemplatives, this necessity of learning and hearing better underlines the importance of allowing ourselves some quiet, some less agitated, moments in which really to hear.

Prayer and Transfiguration

The *electronic church* is a term that has been applied to Sunday morning television and radio evangelists. A viewer reported that on one such program he noticed there was a toll-free number given if you wanted to make a contribution, but a regular pay number if you wanted someone to pray with you. This is probably just another example of how mere things and money so easily outweigh prayer even in the estimation of would-be Christians.

One early Christian source which makes a great effort to give prayer first place is St. Luke's Gospel. St. Luke seldom misses an opportunity to point out that Jesus grounded all his action in prayer. For example, before choosing the twelve apostles: "All night he continued in prayer to God" (6:12). On the occasion of the transfiguration: "And as he was praying, the appearance of his countenance was altered . . ." (9:29). Real insight and transformation, Luke seems to be telling us again and again, come about in prayer or concentrated solitude. Our lack of such insight and our stagnation, the absence of any transfiguration in our lives, may in great part stem from our reluctance to allow time for prayer and quiet. Even before piped-in music came to destroy the possibility of moments of peace, Sören Kierkegaard wrote that we so despise solitude that we can think of nothing better to do with it than use it as a punishment for criminals. In Luke, on the contrary, prayer or reflective solitude, even withdrawal, is the necessary soil from which spring Jesus' deeds or momentous events like his transfiguration.

As is also true for us when we allow time for reflection and prayer, clarity and firmness in decision are the consequences for Jesus. He seems to see more clearly and face with resolve the difficult way that lies before him. And before the event is over, the voice of the Father is heard telling the disciples and us: "This is my Son, my Chosen; listen to him" (9:35). Prayer and listening are correlative.

Both the words of Jesus and the acts of his life, his suffering, death, and resurrection, serve to state what we hear when we truly listen: the Father's love for us is unyielding. It has no off-days. The life and death of Jesus should jolt us into insight about the depth and extent of God's unrelenting love even though the love has always been there. Abraham received it, and all the world before him. In Jesus this love appears with a human face and name.

What has been lacking is nothing on God's side but on our side— receptivity, faith, trust, and confidence. God has never been inaccessible, but our egotism and smallness, our preoccupation with self and self's interests in the narrowest sense, these have made us inaccessible. We turn our backs on love, faith, and trust, and we wallow in gadgets, possessions, trivia, and comfort or more lethally in our all-consuming passion for power, position, and advantage.

If what happens around us and in our world does not seem to be blinding evidence for God's love, that is because we and our fellow citizens of this planet have failed. We are the ones who must make God's love flesh and blood, give it continual reincarnation. Instead of pointing the finger all around us and saying, "I don't see any evidence of his love for the famished and drought-stricken people of Africa or for the lonely old lady down the street," we should turn the finger back on ourselves. A true response from us to God's love would show itself in our using the same ingenuity in feeding the starving or helping the suffering that we now use to make death-dealing missiles or easy-open beer cans.

Our own insight into God's love for us and into its consequences as well as the courage to live them out will come only if we regularly allow a few moments in our life for that insight to grow and gather strength, for trust to develop. Prayer or some prayerful reading of Scripture provides the needed opening for God's love and grace. A resolve to spend a few minutes a day in silence and simple willingness to listen could be the best things we could do for our life in Christ. Public prayer at Mass is essential and serves other purposes, but without the addition of our own unique prayer—not a collection of memorized formulas which we rattle off but something more customized—it runs the risk of being taken for some kind of sacred "rabbit's foot" or amulet.

The strength and awareness gained in prayer are given to us only in order to be given away. Prayer and listening to the word of God give us the conviction and courage to broadcast God's love. We are baptized, we are Christians, not just to add to the church's numbers but to point to the hope that comes from knowing we are in the hands of love.

Again, the Father's love depends for its disclosure on our manifesting it to each other, to the world around us, most likely much more by actions than by words. God does not ordinarily deal with us except through others—we ourselves know his love only because someone else has shown us love or loves us: parents, friends, someone who has helped us in crisis or difficulty. The Father's love and care for the poor, the lonely, the oppressed, the weary, the imprisoned, the weak, and the neglected will become actual through our hands, minds, ingenuity, and effort. Just repeating "Jesus" or "Lord, Lord" can be an easy cop-out excusing us from doing the more demanding witnessing of love, patience, forgiveness, gentleness, faithfulness, sacrifice. The loving Father is announced only to the extent that we show more faith, love, and service.

The prayer or reflective reading of Scripture we have been speaking about, all that listening to the Father's Son, is only the beginning but an irreplaceable foundation for all this. Without it we lack conviction about that love and we lack the strength and the faith to pass it on. May the Holy Spirit, given by Jesus, open our ears to what is, to the meaning of life, and free our tongues to proclaim truth and meaning. So may we be instruments of each other's healing, instruments of God's healing.

Wilted and Weak but Well-off

Maturity consists in the discovery that there comes a critical moment where everything is reversed, after which the point becomes to understand more and more that there is something which cannot be understood.
—SÖREN KIERKEGAARD

You have to understand the meaning of inner peace. A person who has no problems is an idiot. Because a *man* has problems. And the more complicated, the richer he is, the deeper are his problems. . . . In a very deep sense, religion is two things. It is an answer to the ultimate problems of human existence, and it is a challenge to all answers. This is a deep ingredient of existence—problems. And the tragedy of our education today is that we are giving easy solutions: "be complacent; have peace of mind, everything is fine." No! Wrestling is the issue. Facing the challenge is the issue.
—ABRAHAM HESCHEL

Here I am, 58, and I still don't know what I'm going to be when I grow up. —PETER DRUCKER

Man's maturity: to have regained the seriousness that he had as a child at play. —FRIEDRICH NIETZSCHE

For quite some time religious writing and talk has been almost wallowing in the word "community," a sort of religious statement of togetherness. This is unfortunate because community is basically a decent word and concept, vital to Christian living and thought. Being bandied around too much and treated as our *only* ideal it becomes cheap. Similarly in the search for a term more palatable to secularized people than holiness, perfection, or sanctity, we have come up with terms that are often too limited or too egotistic—and certainly overused—such as fulfillment, self-realization, and, with somewhat more dignity and detachment, maturity. In superficial and popular usage maturity is not a bad ideal.

32

Much of our life is seen as a process of maturing, going through stages rooted in nature and abetted by nurture. After a certain point in our personal history we all hope to have our behavior regarded as mature.

My quibble about maturity may come down—not to sour grapes— to an objection to absolutizing any term we use to describe the purpose or end of human development. What we need to be cautioned against is the apparently *finished* and *absolute* maturity that various programs promise. The kind of perfection and release from tension and error they guarantee is just unrealistic and easily leads to severe disillusionment with the whole enterprise of living. Whether assured in the name of religion or pop psychology, this version of maturity seems built on ideas and beliefs simply unjustifiable in terms of common sense and Christian experience and belief.

What I call the illusion of maturity or perfection is compounded of two myths. I use myth here in the popular sense of something false but often widely believed and accepted. As I see them, the two myths are: (1) the myth of complete self-understanding and (2) the myth of self-sufficiency.

By the former I mean the belief that we can, especially with the help of techniques and programs worked out by engineers (maybe plumbers?) of the psyche, know and understand ourselves completely. Our motives, our desires, our faults and virtues appear before us with such clarity that all that remains is to act on the basis of that knowledge to reform and touch up here and there the deficiencies and problems we have discovered. And the result is the spiritual equivalent of Michelangelo's *David*. Implicit in this is a diminished appreciation of a human being which assumes that human nature is as unambiguous—or at least as open to total comprehension—as a blender or an electric typewriter.

> You would play upon me; you would seem to know my stops; you would pluck out the heart of my mystery. . . . Call me what instrument you will, though you can fret me, you cannot play upon me.
>
> *Hamlet*, III, 3

But self-knowledge is not on the same level as knowing how many members made up the original *Rolling Stones* or who succeeded Stalin or how many white corpuscles are necessary for healthy blood.

Experience may have to be added to self-knowledge to convince us that such knowledge is *not* power, i.e., does not of itself lead to improvement. We are neither so clear to others or to ourselves, and when we do come to some genuine self-knowledge, it is likely to lead to at least confusion if not dismay. Self-knowledge is only of some use to us when it is accompanied by some significant reactions on the part of the larger self, reactions involving some judgment of the value of what we find. Simply objective self-knowledge, were that possible, is of no value to us in the process of growing or maturing.

Usually what we do come to know about ourselves does not easily fit into any category that can be communicated through ordinary language. The incommunicability of what we discover when given some insight into ourselves does not absolve us from the effort. To know oneself—no matter how obscure the knowledge—would seem to be a basic responsibility of maturing individuals. To face the resultant fear or anxiety seems also to be a necessary task provided for and faced in the following of Christ.

To have looked into the depths that self-knowledge may open to us, to have seen our weaknesses and strange inclinations—the puzzling contradictions within—should help destroy any illusion of self-sufficiency. We should become aware of our participation in the sin and confusion of the world. What we see or learn of our own insubstantiality, the internal confusion we may see, should leave us possibly a bit wilted, worried, and weak-kneed. Our glimpse of the interior should make us realize that the task of rebuilding life or giving it a substantial scaffolding is beyond our limited creativity and power. Till we experience it to some degree we must take the truth of our insufficiency as a fact which we are not yet ready to face. Ortega y Gasset says, "Life is at the start a chaos in which one is lost." For most of us that may be a reading back of later insight. Our understanding of our participation in the world's sin must come with experience and reflection.

Mercifully and rightly we are allowed to grow and develop with some illusions of power and self-creation. That has its place in our development. But to accept "self-creation" as the last word and to build our spirituality around enhancing such an illusion would be a delusion. Such seems to be the imaginary and theoretical maturity which pop psychology so often suggests we should take for granted as our goal. Certainly, to arrive at some conviction of our insufficiency without enough effort at making our lives—without at some time straining our potential— might easily mean just laziness and minimal understanding. One shouldn't become humble too quickly! Paradoxically, awareness of our insufficiency is only worthwhile if it has been impressed upon us in the wake of some hardy effort at living and working.

If what I have been saying is true, then maturity is no easily charted path from inadequate self-knowledge to perfect self-knowledge. We don't follow some freeway to happiness with our "self," some balance of tensions and desires, some here-and-now nirvana which enables us to smile blandly at the outrages and surprises of life. Rather than leading to reinforcement of our convictions of self-possession and self-control, true understanding leads to some sense of our mystery and even our misery. The greatest exemplars of all this—Augustine, Pascal, Luther, Kierkegaard, etc.—have concluded that their salvation or maturity consisted in abandoning this crazy-mixed-up self to the arms and grace of God. Possibly they appear too much like outsize versions to be helpful to us. They seem to illustrate too perfectly, too loftily, the following of Jesus.

Whether we all can or must or, in fact, do go all the way with these giants of Christian living and thought, it seems to me they tell us something about human maturity that remains applicable even on much smaller scales. Like the extremes and exaggerations of art and artists, the intensities of the saints bring into sharp relief a basic truth. They illustrate that the final word in our maturing is passivity, surrender, relaxing, letting go, faith—call it what we will. Instead of settling for a prepackaged and manageable maturity consisting of systematic steps and stages, they picture maturity ("perfection") as a gift, not an achievement, as a route full of discontinuities, as primarily an attitude of soul rather than a collection of moral and legal requirements, as God's work, not ours.

Before coming back to this side of our development, there remains something else to be said about how half-baked our maturity always is. Obviously we can speak of maturity and finished character quite easily if the criteria are not too high. However, we are not concerned here with cheap accomplishments but with the maturity urged on us by the teaching of Jesus. That maturity means, for example, the absence of ill will and self-aggrandizement at the expense of others, a harmony of desires, possibilities, and capabilities, an ability to respond to events and circumstances in such a way as to utilize them for good. In summary, for Christians, maturity must be centered on the dominance of unselfish love in our lives to the point where, ideally, we act only from love.

But what do we find? The moment of death finds all of us still far from the ideal of total Christian maturity: bits and pieces of ill will, sensual grasping, irrational intransigence, resentment, self-pity, untrusting anxiety, self-importance, shortness of temper and patience, petty pride, etc. Who does not recognize how much some one or the other or several of these and similar faults persist through all the other changes of our life; how some defect first noticed in adolescense is still with us today; how petulance remains almost as persistent as an allergy? Popular belief and theology have always understood this. Popular Catholic belief has often presumed that the way to eternal happiness inevitably went through some purgatory, some purification. Prayers and Masses for the dead are built around the same belief. And today, when belief in hell is at its nadir, purgatory or the equivalent is finding a better press, new support, and new champions in theologians outside the Catholic tradition. The idea that most of us at the moment of death are just too imperfect for union with God, that we are not enough like him to live with him, urges a number of theologians to see in a less pictorial purgatory an expectable necessity for the ordinary mortal. The evidence for the persistence of characterological flaws is everywhere; honest self-examination can easily supply the details.

Is the tenor of all this a sort of counsel to despair? Not at all. Rather, the persistence of our failings, the imperfect quality of our so-called maturing, only tell us that the calculated and planned maturity of the how-to books and of Christian moralism is doomed to be illusory, if not impossible of achievement. Why must it be doomed? Because as the Gospel tells us, maturity is a gift, not an achievement. We don't save ourselves; Jesus is the Savior. Our failures serve the useful purpose of throwing us back more forcefully on God. They reiterate the lesson of the ultimate importance of surrender, passivity—lessons so contrary to salvation *a la* Adam or Ayn Rand. Our final inadequacy teaches us at least to relax a bit and to realize that the responsibility of our perfection is not meant to be shouldered by ourselves alone—that egotistical spiritual development, spiritual body-building, is not the point of human existence.

Much of the painful historical discussion within Christianity about faith and works has revolved around this problem. The Reformation protest centered to a great degree on efforts to clarify the belief that we're saved by the action of God and not by painstaking spiritual craftsmanship on our part. From Genesis through the New Testament there is a continual stream of warning that trying to be gods is the surest way of falling completely and despairingly on our faces.

Someone Else Is Concerned

Another way of saying this is to recognize that alongside the dire prophetic warnings about "shaping up" there is also the message of Jesus about relying on the Father, knowing that he is concerned about every aspect of our life. What can our anxiety do about increasing our height? Look at the birds of the air and the flowers of the field, Jesus says. True, we seem to be more able to control elements of our life than they are, but, that passage from the Gospels urges, we are also, like them, part of the created world and, unlike them, able to consciously trust in God's care.

The message is not: Relax, everything's okay; you're just great as you are. But rather: Relax, because he made us, he knows our faults and efforts, and he forgives. He is able to work in us in ways not accessible to our conscious speculation or imagination. His concern for our development is coupled with power to do something about it. He has given us a Savior: being saved requires of us more reliance on him rather than anxious concern about tidying up every corner of our private plot.

In all this, there is the necessity for some prudence, some judgment. Elsewhere I maintained that we come to perceive the limitations of reason best through a decent and sufficiently strenuous use of that faculty. So here this relaxing in the care of the Savior is only decent and legitimate to the degree that we have taken growth and spiritual development seriously. Maybe we need the judgment of a spiritual guide or, if that sounds too pretentious, of someone we deem fairly balanced who can tell us when we're digging into the windowsill too desperately with our fingernails in the effort to hang on to our self-salvation. There is a time for everything: to discern the moment and situation for this ultimate letting-go probably requires some outside counsel as well as personal analysis.

Or is it a matter of observing a certain rhythm here? Not only in some ultimate sense must we rely on God, relax in his grace and care, but all along, in each particular struggle, there need to be moments when we do not resign our ideal but understand that it is also someone else's concern too. To grasp that—in almost every area of our life—we are always going to retain an unfinished character (despite, sometimes, the superlative judgment of friendly observers) is, once again, just to recognize our limited creatureliness. So what's new, where's the surprise? Maturity, the catchword we started all this with, includes an acceptance of the fact that part of our adjustment to truth and reality is some willingness to see that ultimate responsibility is not simply ours. William James writes of this—in regard to the more dramatic cases to which we have alluded but nevertheless with some real value for all of us:

> The transition from tenseness, self-responsibility, and worry to equanimity, receptivity, and peace, is the most wonderful of all those shiftings of inner equilibrium, those changes of the personal center of energy, which I have analyzed so often; and the chief wonder of it is that it so often comes about, not by doing, but by simply relaxing and throwing the burden down. The

abandonment of self-responsibility seems to be the fundamental act in specifically religious, as distinguished from moral practice.

Varieties of Religious Experience, 233.

An interesting note in that last and vital sentence is the distinction between religious and moral practice, something worth much more time than we shall be giving it here. It simply implies the secondary character of our actions compared to the more basic matter of our relation to God, the direction of our aspirations. That we are sons and daughters of God through Christ, that we have a Father on whom we can rely, that we are buried with Christ in order to live a risen life with him, that our dignity consists in worshiping and praising the Creator by our use of his gifts: all these are the most important realities of our spiritual life, not a collection of moral commands. This is probably hard to take for many of us educated in the moralistic ambience of American religion, Protestant or Catholic. Not only is this ultimate trust and confidence in God the last word, it is also the initial word. *From it flow* the behavior and moral efforts to which we give so much attention. And Christian tradition argues through some of its more brilliant examples that moral integrity follows the more inevitably the more a solid relation to God is realized and given first place in our consciousness. Be what you already are.

To sum up, a rare bit of theology by Hermann Hesse is relevant here. The scheme he offers is found in an essay entitled "A Bit of Theology" (in *My Belief, Essays on Life and Art*, ed. Theodore Ziolkowski, trans. Denver Lindley [Farrar, Straus & Giroux, 1974] 189-201.) Resistant as he seemed to be to systems and formulations, Hesse nevertheless thought that in the world's religions there was a discernible pattern for the spiritual life. He saw three stages in human development: (1) A state of innocence and irresponsibility, the situation of the young human before the advent of full consciousness and reflection. (2) A period when commands or moral demands of some sort (the law, society, the world, etc.) show up our inability to live up totally to what is expected. This in turn produces guilt or a sense of failure. (3) The third stage, our reaction to the second, is either despair (giving up, declaring the whole worth nothing, adopting a cynical hopelessness toward life) or faith. The latter is, in Hesse's view, a confidence and trust that God cares and will accomplish what to us seems impossible. His most helpful definition of this faith is a "higher irresponsibility." We started out, according to his scheme, with the infantile, youthful state of *given* irresponsibility, a pre-conscious state; we end up with a *willed* recovery of that "irresponsibility" based on a realization that vis-à-vis the Father, we are ultimately children who must depend on him for the actualization of our goals. God wishes to bring us to a maturity which is identical with becoming once again a child.

Once More with Thinking

There is nothing conventional, neat, or altogether logical about a crucifixion or the Church. Conversion in Christ involves broken hearts more than changes of mind.   —AIDAN KAVANAGH, O.S.B.

What you have inherited from your fathers,
Acquire it to make it yours.   —GOETHE

If we are worth anything at all, we still have to undergo one or several conversions. The transition from a traditionalist and middle-class piety to a genuinely Christian life—that is to say, to the life of humility and of charity—is at least as painful as the transition from atheism to faith.
—EMMANUEL MOUNIER

Those of us who have heard even perfunctorily the Sunday Scripture readings are familiar with the criticism Jesus makes of the religion of his fellow Jews. He warns them that prostitutes, tax collectors, and Samaritans will more easily enter God's presence than they. We readily take such passages as appropriate, confirming as they do *our* conception of Hebraic religion as exclusivist and self-satisfied. It was to be expected, we feel, that *it* would shut out various classes and types of people from all hope of salvation. *We* know better; God wills the good of all peoples. Similarly, we may be willing to see the application of all this to Christians, Catholics, at least of the past. They too have been smug, sure of having arrived.

But this is all too facile, of course. Our acquiescence in Jesus' severe judgment may be rooted in an insufficiently conclusive attachment to Christianity, to the following of Christ. We affect such an unfastened relationship to our religion that we find it incredible that being a Christian could be cause for some special self-congratulation. We feel very liberated from the Catholicism of the past which, apparently, along

40

with some types of Protestantism, insisted that there was no salvation outside the church. But if that is our stance, then, of course, Christ is offering *us* no real challenge in these censorious passages. They have become really obsolete or apply only to a few anachronistic Bible thumpers and old-style Catholics. The whole matter of why one should be a Christian rather than a humanist, a Catholic rather than a devotee of some guru, etc., is more than enough for another essay. The point here is that I am writing for people who continue in whatever way "in the church"—people capable at least of being tempted to some self-satisfaction, tempted to feel that this adhesion has some special value. If our religious commitment is too free-floating and fluid, then, of course, an inclination to complacency is a contradiction in terms.

Repeatedly Jesus demands that we come to a decision, that we don't sit on the fence, that we risk believing. If our response is to have any teeth, it must be a commitment with some concreteness about it, involving a specific tradition, some practice and belief, some consequences. A benign and genial affection for Jesus usually leaves us quite undisturbed. The ecumenical movement properly understood would not be taken by most who have thought about it to have negated genuine commitment in favor of just being "open" to all faiths, all traditions, all people of good will. That may easily be but another way of avoiding a response to Jesus' call for a decision. Also, it seems to me that serious ecumenists do not suggest that we attempt to short-circuit the movement toward unity by junking necessarily pointed commitments in favor of an amorphous and seriously reduced Christianity. Rather, they see that unity will depend on Christians of various backgrounds being sincerely devoted to and understanding the type of Christianity to which they are committed. By living out the best in diverse tradition we are more likely to meet ultimately where the good and the true in them all converge.

For most of us, our relation to Christ, the church, Christianity, began with our baptism as infants. Our subsequent history may have been varied but often it has meant an implicit acceptance of belief in Jesus Christ as a more or less tribal matter, something done with varying degrees of fervor and conviction. Often we are Catholics, it would seem, for the same reasons that we are Irish, Italian, or German—it's all part of the package. When a grown member of the family rejects or abandons that faith it is regarded as equivalent to spurning one's heritage and family. Despite all the praise of united families, family and religion may at a certain juncture of our life be too closely allied.

It seems increasingly necessary that Christians make their own the religion they were given by the care of parents and the power of baptism.

Why "increasingly necessary"? The support and ties of the family tend to be more and more nominal in our age. Mobility in terms of vocation and where one will live deprives us often of the support and pressure that close family ties have meant so frequently. A secularized world seems to put on the individual the burden and responsibility of choosing and defining his or her own commitment about how to live and for what purpose, with little reinforcement from the environing society.

More positively, it is only appropriate that educated adults do not simply accept without question or reflection an inherited set of religious beliefs, practices, and customs. The suggestion that such traditions should be questioned and appraised by no means presumes that they will be found unworthy of acceptance. It is merely being argued that such acceptance, if it is to be, should be more human, i.e., flow more from the conscious and willed engagement of the whole person and all that person's faculties. Moreover, shouldn't we suppose that God himself is more honored by an adhesion that is voluntary and mature? Charles Peguy writes somewhere of God asking for the worship and adoration of free human beings, not slaves, of people under no compulsion, no matter how genial, to praise him. We must presume that no more than the rest of us does God want enforced friendship and love. Parents must be made happy when they see their grown sons and daughters reverse the centrifugal tendencies of the teens and voluntarily and with pleasure return to visit the family and home.

All this is no argument against infant baptism. There are, it seems to me, many good reasons for continuing it or something similar. Rather, I am saying that faith in Jesus Christ should be consciously affirmed, one's baptism freely ratified when one is old enough to think about it and evaluate it; that it deserves the concentration we bring to subjects like our vocation and marriage. We have little choice about the weak ankles inherited from our mother's side of the family or the curly hair rampant among ourselves and other relatives of the Donahue side, but belief in Jesus should be for all of us some sort of personal response to his constant challenges and calls which we hear in the Gospels.

The baptism of an infant points up the gratuitousness of God's love (i.e., that it is a free, undeserved gift); it tells us that God's love envelopes us independently of our ability or even our willingness to respond—a persistent theme of all of Scripture. By baptism we are made the recipients of God's love or, put another way, baptism is a sign of, among other things, God's desire to save us, that his intention toward us is all for our good. The fact that he loves all human beings is made more pointed. In baptism he says: "I love Hank Smith, Allison Hart, etc." And throughout Scripture there is the strong reiteration that our being saved from chaos, death, and evil is primarily God's work, not ours.

Yet coupled with all that is, even in such a strong apologist for belief in salvation-as-a-free-gift as St. Paul, an insistence on our response. It is St. Paul who reminds us so often and eloquently that if we are to rise with Christ and reign with him, we must die with him, share his cross and death. And that is what the adult commitment to Christ means: an affirmation that I will live my life in accordance with the pattern lived and hallowed by Jesus. It will be a life of death to narrow self-seeking and sin and a constant willingness to rise to new life, to live for God. Though God loves us prior to our loving him and independently of it (that is the mystery, for instance, of the "chosen" people), our reply and the ensuing relationship engaging all of our powers is expected throughout the Scriptures.

Here is where the fashionable "born-again" (didn't all three presidential candidates recently declare themselves "born-again"?) crowd are surely correct. Baptism does ask of us a yes or no, a spiritual rebirth entailing a resolution to turn from narcissistic concerns to the wider life of service to God and others. For some of us, the adult "finding of Jesus" will be a real resurrection from a life of sensuality, pride, selfishness, and heedlessness to a totally new orientation, a real "conversion." For others it will be a moving from an unquestioning, possibly somewhat bovine, acceptance of what family milieu gave us to a more energetic and intelligent embracing of what it means to be a Christian. There may be no dramatic changes in behavior but a distinct revision of outlook and intention.

Unfortunately some of the popular apostles of this rebirth in our age have all the worst qualities of religious imperialists of any age or milieu: they prescribe exactly how this rebirth must take place, the degree of emotion required to certify its genuineness, and the formula which proves it has taken. Usually it must be "I accept the Lord Jesus Christ as my personal Savior" or some slight variant on that. It has even been treated in writing on the level of a book on how to grow orchids in your window box or how to see Iraq on a camel and $5 a day—someone has written *How To Be Born Again*. There is some small comfort in all this for those still smarting from oversystematization and overregulation in the Catholic tradition. It demonstrates that the old Catholic temptation to package the whole matter and systematize it to death is, after all, more than an "old Catholic" temptation. It is a basic hazard of religion in general. Against such imperialists we need to be convinced that God is great enough to work in a unique way in each of us and that there is no one simple path for every follower of Jesus or would-be follower. That we should ratify our baptism or junk the whole thing may be clear but *how* you or I do it is a very individual matter and no one should presume to dictate the style and pace.

For some, the turn to a more fully Christian life will be a slow and gradual growing into an appreciation of what parents taught or Sister Equilibria said way back in the fifth grade; a recognition that all that old stuff contains priceless help about how to live. Such people find themselves, by dint of conscientiousness, openness, and persistent prayer, often quietly, without any big-band accompaniment, being convinced that they must live for Jesus Christ by a life of unselfishness and service. Some few, like John Wesley and others, may be able to date their spiritual rebirth to 5:03 P.M., July 23, 1977, standing before the butter brickle in Pontiac's ice cream fountain. But I think we fool ourselves and, worse yet, others if we think and proclaim such exciting, localized, instantaneous, and tear-filled changes of heart as usual or necessary.

Maybe we can return now to the Samaritans, prostitutes, and tax collectors. The necessary adult decision to live the Christian life always remains a matter that should be open to criticism and reevaluation, all the more if dramatic and emotional features lend it a definitive-appearing character. The liturgy realistically provides for a yearly rededication— through Lent and the Easter Vigil specifically—to living the risen life of Christ. Jesus' insistence that so many of the "wrong" people will enter the kingdom tells us that faith knows no simple, clear boundaries and that there are no automatic guarantees of its completeness. We are allowed no complacency because we have dedicated ourselves to living for Christ, because we say "Lord, Lord" or "Jesus is Lord" any more than we were by wearing a Miraculous Medal or the brown scapular. Our weekly envelopes (unfortunately seen by an occasional pastor as the infallible sign of predestination), the nine First Fridays, or the fifty-two Sundays: none of these confirms our reservation on a cozy chair by the fire in some club called the kingdom of God.

The true following of Christ does not allow us any magical security, whether our decision to live in the pattern of the death and rising of Jesus has been made in the privacy of our own heart or proclaimed before thousands in the Oakland coliseum. The Protestant Reformation rightly insisted that the church needs constant reform; equally each of its members needs to renew his or her following of Jesus. Lapses, losing fervor, failures, and gross returns to our worst vices all tell us we need to begin again, renew our commitment, that it is never finished. Our flops and falls don't deny the value of some memorable moment in which it all became clear; that time of conversion still serves as a high-water mark, an indication of what grace and decision can do in us. Our failures are also an insurance against the simplistic and un-Christian notion that our will is all that is needed. "Where there's a will, there's a way" seems incompatible with biblical Christianity.

In his rule for monasteries, St. Benedict required of his monks not the vows of chastity, obedience, and poverty (a later formulation) but other vows including an all-encompassing vow promising effort at transformation of one's morals, a promise to work for continual improvement of life. Experience had undoubtedly taught him that self-love, idolatry, insensitivity, and self-righteousness are not easily uprooted but are about as avoidable as red tape, crabgrass, and piped-in music.

Living or Waiting?

There are so many things that we wish we had done yesterday, so few that we feel like doing today.   —MIGNON MCLAUGHLIN

I had an evangelist friend in college. He operated on a shoestring, but one day drove up in a brand new Chrysler. We asked him where he got the money, and he replied, "I'm still broke. I managed to eke out a down payment, but according to my charts, Jesus is coming back before I have to make the payments."   —*Connexion*

"What'll we do with ourselves this afternoon?" cried Daisy, "and the day after that, and the next thirty years?"   —F. SCOTT FITZGERALD

The unhappy waiters and killers of time, . . . students who can't be happy until they've graduated, servicemen who can't be happy until they're discharged, single folk who can't be happy until they're married, workers who can't be happy until they're retired, adolescents who can't be happy until they're grown, ill people who can't be happy until they're well, failures who can't be happy until they succeed, restless people who can't be happy until they get out of town; and, in most cases, vice versa, people waiting, waiting for the world to begin.   —TOM ROBBINS

Hal Lindsey and his wife, despite his *The Late Great Planet Earth*—which preaches the imminent end of the world—have invested a substantial part of their earnings in long-term real estate transactions. Other earnings went into those here-and-now Rolls Royces the Lindseys sport.
—*Presbyterian Journal*

Owing to lack of technological development, the people of biblical times were denied the blessings of disaster movies. Apart from authentic cataclysm, which seems to have hit them often enough, their nearest substitute may have been the type of literature we hear read in each year's late fall liturgy. In this type (genre) of literature called *apocalyptic,*

46

peculiar to Jewish writing of the time, the stars fall from the skies, the moon turns to blood, the sun is darkened, etc. But, unlike such cinematic landmarks as *Towering Inferno* and *Jaws*, works of this type were produced, not to enliven an otherwise predictable life with a little fright ("an oasis of horror in a desert of ennui" was Baudelaire's phrase), but to remind the readers that no matter how bad things might get through war, catastrophe, and persecution, God was with them and would have the last victorious word.

"Wars, earthquakes, famine, omens in the sky, were part of the standard stock-in-trade, the stylistic devices, of this type of writing" and were the setting for Yahweh's message of consolation and hope. "Attempts to interpret them as references to specific events in the first century are a waste of time" (*Interpreter's Bible*), and all the more useless are the efforts to see the course of Russian-American relations for the next several decades in these ancient pages. The point of such texts, valid for all ages, is that even if heaven and earth should fold up and pass away, God's word and the love it proclaims are irrevocable: nothing can alter them.

Despite their lack of that concrete application so beloved of fundamentalists of every period, these texts do refer generally to the future, to a time when God will roll up the scroll of history and the Lord will return. They are heavy with looming events and injunctions to alertness and watchfulness. This imminence struck many of the early Christians so strongly that they expected God to ring down the final curtain during their lifetime. When the decades rolled on and this did not happen, they recognized that "of that day or that hour no one knows, not even the angels in heaven, nor even the Son, but only the Father" (Mark 13:32). Eventually they conceded that the last day might be far off in the future, but they and their heirs to the Christian tradition maintained a stress on an impending coming through such celebrations as Advent.

One is entitled to wonder whether or not they and we ourselves have overlooked the likelihood that the return of the Lord is frequent, ordinary. As Teilhard de Chardin suggests, we may still and wrongly put the second coming, the parousia, too much in some cataclysmic event of the future, all the while (1) missing the constant breaking-in of Christ into our lives and (2) failing to do our part to forward or clarify the presence of the Lord.

Be that as it may, it is undeniable that Christianity remains in many ways oriented to the future. Especially in Catholic Christianity this has taken the form in the fairly recent past of regarding the present world and this life as an anteroom to the real mansion, the life to follow. And,

I think it *is* clear that the Christian tradition in its fullness does not allow us to give absolute value to our life on this earth, in this age. Some ultimate deliverance from evil and death is central to Christian belief. Another movement in Christian thought and practice has secularized this looking to the future and, while keeping the emphasis there, has made that future part of world history, i.e., has postulated a time in human history when, through the actualization of Christ's teaching in sufficient numbers of people and societies, justice and love will have transformed our world.

No matter how we view it or picture it, the future is with us now and is always inextricably bound up with faith and hope. Even apart from religion, the future is essential to the dynamics of any human life. Both in the long run and on a shorter scale there is no getting away from the pull of the future, from the incentive it provides, the energizing it effects. Goals and ideals beckon us on: the realization of either a vocation or a vacation can keep us going. Almost inescapably we live in anticipation of skiing in January or a happy Christmas, a summer away, a weekend break. Little needs to be added about this future in which and for which we all live so unavoidably.

What needs a word more often within the context of Christian life is the *present*, the here and now. Our commitment to the future or to eternity, coupled with prophetic prodding about a more just world, something we share with Judaism, makes us feel guilty if we talk about living in the present. Needless to say, those whose Christianity has lost all coloring suffer from the opposite difficulty: their whole vision is narrowed down to the present moment. Living in the present is equated with hedonism, living it up, forgetfulness of tomorrow or of eternity. But "eat, drink, and be merry" is a parody of true and full living in the present and that "tomorrow you die" oversimplifies the rationale.

The apocalyptic texts referred to in the beginning of this essay stress imminence and urge watchfulness. A few words now about the latter. Though we seem to forget it all too easily, the best form of readiness may not be a retreat to the kneeler but sticking to the tasks of the moment. Though we often think of eternity as following time, Christian tradition is strong on the fact that eternity is rooted in the quality of our present life. It grows out of a life lived generously here and now in love and service. "Anyone who eats my flesh, . . . who believes in me"—can we not add: anyone who loves family and friends, who does good work, who enjoys the beauty of creation?—"*has* eternal life."

Scripture records Paul's reaction when he heard that his converts were concluding that since the Lord was returning, it was useless to repair the roof or change the oil. They would idle the engine and wait. He responded, "Now concerning the coming of our Lord Jesus Christ . . . , we beg you . . . not to be quickly shaken in mind or excited, either by spirit or by word, or by letter purporting to be from us, to the effect that the day of the Lord has come" (2 Thess 2:1-2). The fact that Christ will return somehow, sometime, is no excuse for putting the car in park. More baldly, Paul said, Those who won't work, won't eat. Life has to be lived, work done, friends cared for, promises kept. Hope remains intrinsic to being a Christian. But no more than we can live simply in the past should we try to live totally in the future: neither should outweigh the present. The Eucharist itself, around which Christian life is built, is no mere matter of nostalgic recalling of the past or anticipation of the glorious future but a making *present* of the offering and meal of the Lord for us who live now and for our purposes.

The future, eternity, our hopes, come to reality only on the heels of our present steps. Better yet, like happiness, they may very well come the more surely they are forgotten in attention to the perfecting of the present moment and our task in it. Alertness and readiness are served and a good life lived when we are as totally present to this moment and task as is possible. If we love God best not by some condescending love of others "for his sake" but in themselves, for their own God-willed good, so we serve him not by looking ahead to the reward we are acquiring—or back to the failures and successes of the past—but by working and living in the present wholeheartedly and generously. That is not the same as being swept along heedlessly by circumstances; it presumes some choices and decisions based on our values and our ends. Once they are sure and firm, we more easily live in the present. "Love and do what you will" does presume that the love is of a high order of selflessness. Similarly, living in the present is not an enterprise unrelated to our goals and the meaning of our life.

Both our culture and our religion have given the future great prominence, and with some justification. Still it cannot be overemphasized that we are very poor at living in the present. "We look before and after and pine for what is not; our sincerest laughter with some pain is fraught . . . " was written probably a century ago and remains a valid description of so much of our life. As these lines from Shelley's "To a Skylark" (XVIII) say, our present is muddled by our inability to be really in it, by thought of what might have been or where we could be. "There is nothing rarer in life than that single moment in which we have no desire to be elsewhere" (Mauriac). But real life is here with this family, in this job, in this month, in this place—at least while we're here.

If we're convinced we can do it better in Marin County, then maybe we should move there rather than impoverish life here in Schenectady or Walhalla. But even then, before we make this questionable move, we might attempt to realize the wisdom of the old saws about being able to change the skies but not the heart. Will we be better able to live here and now if we change the here and now? There *is* life after high school if we let go of high school and adolescence. There *is* life here and now if, instead of saving our best efforts for some uncertain existence as a business tycoon or as some improbable combination of Nelson Rockefeller, Elton John, and Robert Redford, we would give our energy and our attention to this work, this moment, these people, this place, this me. If we think life is always around the corner—geographically or chronologically— we soon find there are no corners. We're on a circular track.

To let ourselves think that real life is elsewhere at some other time can be nothing but a ploy to avoid ever facing life. Whether we're going to stop drinking, start dancing, study the Gospels, or take up swimming, now is the time. Existence in the here and now is its own reward, an antidote to the depression brought on by worry and thought about the future or the past, and it is the only beginning possible for some better future.

"If your work bores you, try doing it well." Doing our work or carrying out our resolves, listlessly or half-heartedly or sloppily, prolonging the orientation program indefinitely, with an eye on the clock or the calendar—all amount to shadowboxing with life, dancing around the ring and never coming to blows. Life becomes a constant rehearsal with no opening night. A Zen saying puts the right approach well: "When walking just walk, when sitting just sit. Above all, don't wobble!" The drudgery of any work or existence is so often due to allowing it to be accompanied by regrets about the past or useless worries about the future.

Though we associate this whole matter of living here and now with Eastern religions and movements like Zen, it could be shown that it is a strong strand in Western and Christian thought also. Let one example from a classic source suffice:

> We are never satisfied with the present; we only use the present to arrange the future. We so neglect the present that it and the past only serve as means to some unsure future. And so we never live, but only hope to live; and as we are always preparing to be happy, it is inevitable that we should never actually be happy.
>
> Blaise Pascal, *Pensees*

There are and have been in Christian tradition people who do live here and now, with their whole heart; they are, in fact, more important than those we might cite who have written on or thought about the issue.

When they are a bit spectacular we call them saints. God himself does not ask more of us than this: to live from our greatest depths, from our talents and health, utilizing even our peculiarities for God and for others, for that unfolding of Christ in us which is the realization of our true self.

Possibly only a religion that tells us we know neither the day nor the hour urges us sufficiently to live *now:* possibly only a religion that has traditionally urged us to face up to the fact of death can give us the strength to get behind the cosmetics and drugs to the real human condition. Some time ago an ad for watches priced from $125 to $1,595 boasted, "Other watches only record time, Brand Such and Such dignifies time." We can go through life just recording time, ticking it off by always being partially absent in the past or the future or in another place. Or we can truly dignify it by taking every passing moment as infinitely valuable, capable here and now of beginning the life, love, and joy of eternity.

The Great Christian Platitude

To make the reality of God present; this is the essential mystery of Jesus.
—GUNTHER BORNKAMM

To say that love is God is romantic idealism. To say that God is love is either the last straw or the ultimate truth.   —FREDERICK BUECHNER

The deepest motive for believing is the awareness of being loved by God. What first brings a person to faith is a sense that God has grasped one at the depths of life, reaching out somehow from the cross of Christ to secure one in love. Feeling this, one lays down disbelief and becomes a believer. What keeps that person believing is the experience of being held, controlled, subdued and surrounded by God's love.   —LEWIS SMEDES

"In the eyes of a lover pockmarks are dimples." So goes a Japanese proverb. An equivalent Ukrainian one says: "Love tells us many things that are not so." Our more commonplace version of the same is, of course, "Love is blind." Proverbs condense into a few words something true if not downright obvious. Occasionally they're catchy; more often they're simply trite. "Haste makes waste." "A glutton digs his grave with his teeth." "Time heals all." "God is love." "A penny saved is a penny earned." "He fasts enough that has a bad meal." "All work and no play makes Jack a dull boy." And so on.

"God is love" is in that list because, unfortunately, for most of us it resonates with about the same excitement and revelatory power as "Haste makes waste." Endless, careless, and cheap repetition have made it stale and neutralized its impact. But the Scripture writers do not throw that statement around with the glib abandon of those who provide the texts for greeting cards and posters. It occurs only once in the whole New Testament and that in the First Letter of St. John, chapter 4, verses 8, 9, and 16.

52

In writing this, St. John is not offering us some cosmic generalization. It is clear that he is writing in the context of the life and work of Jesus Christ. "God is love" (i.e., love is his basic and enduring attitude toward us, is behind all that befalls us and is unaffected by anything we might do). We know God is love, he tells us, only because God has sent his Son to save us from sin and death. The actual words of the text are: "In this the love of God was made manifest among us, that God sent his only Son into the world, so that we might live through him" (v. 9). Our conclusive proof, evidence, that God is infinitely loving in his disposition toward us is not to be found in nature, life, or human experience, but in the extraordinary intervention of God in history which culminated in the suffering, death, and resurrection of his Son. So often, sloppily and sentimentally, we toss off remarks about how nature proclaims the goodness, even love, of God. Yet, at best, nature is a most ambiguous witness to a loving God. No respectable philosopher could ever propose "God is love" as an empirically verifiable statement about the universe.

At times, of course, we do find nature, life, and other people revealing God to us. And ultimately, as our faith grows that should become the rule, a frequent occurrence. John is, in a sense, justifying that. His point is that the only decisive bit of evidence that we have for God's irrevocable love for us and, consequently, for seeing it all around us, is in the life and work of Jesus Christ. It is not a self-evident truth like the eventual return of spring or the fact that humans are born of humans. Nature does not always or inevitably, apart from our faith, tell all the world that God is loving and concerned. How does the devastation of an earthquake, a flash flood, cancer—how do any of these confirm that God is loving? Or our more specifically human experiences: How does God's love show itself to or in a child born without arms or with an incurable disease? How does it show itself to a person whose background and milieu pretty well guarantee that he or she will never know a day with enough to eat?

And cynics have spoken the feelings of all of us in objecting to any absolute trust we might put in our fellow human beings. Family and friends may heal our wounds, console us, and be with us, we hope, in tragedy. On the other hand, there are parents who make enemies look good. There is child abuse and desertion, betrayal and unfaithfulness. There are friends who find that they can do without friendship when their advancement is involved; others may turn on us in mental illness or passion. Not all fathers, mothers, and friends are mirrors of a loving God.

Certainly nature, life, and friends do give us days when we can say with another old proverb, "Life is just a bowl of cherries." It's spring;

you're in love; there's enough cash for a fishing trip to British Columbia and Amoco has personally guaranteed that you will have all the gas you'll ever need. Not only is it a nice world; not only is God clearly love; he seems to have a crush on you. But at other times—if not in the past, then surely in the future—winters seem endless, everything goes wrong, every relationship turns sour, disaster clings to you like a deer fly. Then we say, "Nature is cruel" and "People are no darn good" and "Life is the pits." We ask, God is love? Indeed, reflecting on the vicissitudes of human life, a fair number of philosophers have concluded that if there is a God he must be cruel or insane.

One more kindly philosopher approached it differently. Speaking from a non-biblical and not specifically religious framework, that genial genius William James said that we are all faced with the problem of our basic attitude or stance vis-à-vis the universe and/or its author. He thought we had four basic options: (1) We survey our world and conclude that we do not yet have enough evidence to draw any conclusions about whether or not we're the object of hate or love; therefore we refrain from acting. (2) Or, we decide that the whole enterprise is not to be trusted; we give up on it and let it go to hell, so to speak. (3) Or, we trust the powers that be and do our best, in spite of the risk that the universe may fail. (4) Or, finally, we flounder by doing one thing one day and another the next. From the vantage point of his pragmatism, James concluded that to trust that there is some good sense and benevolence operating in the universe (3) is, in practice, the best thing to believe. Only such a conviction can impel us to the good and purposeful action that life requires, can motivate us for a life that is satisfying and productive.

John the Evangelist is telling us that God, as might have been expected, foresaw our problem and understood that in the midst of so many conflicting signals we would have difficulty in getting up in the morning (someone has written that faith is what gets you out of bed in the morning) and that we would find it hard to live consistently for anything. To act, or even simply to avoid despair, requires that we have some assurance that God is much more than just indifferent to our status. An unalterable conviction that God is love can rest only on our belief that Jesus Christ, the Son of God made man, suffered, died, and rose for us and that through him we have the assurance that he is with us as we go through the first two and will bring us to the third. Circumstances and evidence that is as shifting as the stock market, currency exchange rates, the weather, our blood pressure or cholesterol level, do not provide anything on which to build a faith.

Our trust that God is love is founded on his initiative in calling us friends and in allowing his son to suffer and die on our behalf. On his part, he has ruled out the possibility of a divorce. Nor are we talking about a springtime romance that fades with the last lilac or that can be killed by our bad breath. It will persist, he has assured us, through whatever little horrors we may come up with in our personal lives: our coldness to others and their needs; our self-destruction through drink, work, drugs; our prostitution of our persons and talents for momentary satisfaction or gain; our disloyalty and forgetfulness of God himself for long periods. Through all this and beyond, he is there, the incorrigible lover, the one Andrew Greeley calls the madly generous Father who just won't stop. After everyone else has thrown up their hands, he still expects something new and good from us.

With that—the love, generosity, and hope that such love can sustain and inspire—we come to the most immediate effect of all this. If we are to believe in and properly love ourselves, if we are to believe in and trust and love others, some such rock-ribbed love must uphold us. "Only he who is already loved can love, only he who has been trusted can trust, only he who has been an object of devotion can give himself" (Bultmann). One of the banal proverbs quoted earlier receives a more profound application here. God's love for us is not only blind but deaf to our stupidities and sin, so ready is he to forgive, to expect the new and good from us.

Once More with Hope

At life's each call the heart must be prepared to take its leave and to commence afresh courageously and with no hint of grief submit itself to other and newer ties. A magic dwells in each beginning and protecting us it tells us how to live.   —HERMANN HESSE

. . . but one has to see and recognize that life is threatened radically in order to grasp what God is and wants to be for us. It is only then that one can believe and hope and grasp God's promises in the good news of Jesus Christ.   —KARL RAHNER

For some of us believe that God is almighty and *may* do all; and that he is all-wisdom and can do all; but that he is all-love, and will do all—there we fail. It is this unknowing that most holdeth back God's lovers, as I see it.   —JULIAN OF NORWICH

To accept and to endure with patience and with trust in an ever greater God and his grace the difference between what we are and what we should be is itself a positive task for Christians. A correct acceptance indeed always includes an attempt to overcome this difference in an upward direction, and hence it includes a "no" to something and a "yes" to something else and better.   —KARL RAHNER

The important passages of Scripture are never given to us merely to tell us something interesting or informative about David or Eve or even Jesus. Ultimately—that is, at some time in our life, if they are attended to well enough—they will be found to contain a challenge to us, to our way of living, to our attitudes. If may take years for a particular passage to do that for me or for another. We cannot force its power or "relevance." Even one who preaches the word or writes about it can only attempt to open it for others but never claim to have decisively done that. Repeated exposure to the word of God in the liturgy, in the company of others, and in our own reading, reflection, and study, is the sole and often slow way to enter into it. The recurrence of the same texts at Mass (now happily exposing us to more and varied texts) is just for this purpose: to allow the message to sink in gradually, to find its appropriate moment in our lives. The mystery or obscurity of Scripture is really its depth; it deals with human situations too deep for the same words we use to talk about the density of bread or steel, the quality of the air, or the sound of a jet.

One such endless source of mystery and wonderment is given us in the account of the temptation of Jesus in the desert with its accompanying background in the Hebrew Scriptures. I would emphasize *endless* here because what follows is at most one fragment of the mystery, one way of looking at this many-sided event.

In the story of the devil's temptation of Jesus (Matt 4:1-11) the inciter to evil suggests that Jesus (1) turn stones into bread, (2) throw himself off a high point of the temple, and (3) worship the devil.

Jesus says no to the temptation to use his power to produce the equivalent of a couple of Big Macs in the desert. He says no to the suggestion that he do a circus act. And he says no to the offer of instant kingship in place of the cross that will lead him to resurrection. Put this way, the temptations of Jesus emphasize that the devil was urging him to showy, trivial, and debasing uses of his power, to give in to the desire for immediate success. That lesson *alone* has extraordinary significance today when so many are tempted by offers of instant success, peace, integrity, or serenity.

But his no to temptation has even broader importance. It means something for us who are not tempted to pull Spiderman stunts and do not have the world offered to us at the top of the John Hancock Building. It says something to our temptations to revenge, to some easy and lucrative dishonesty, some cheap use of another person. The Gospel account, as if a reversal of the famous temptation of Adam and Eve, tells us that the outcome of such a trial, of our trials, does not have to be defeat. In the Genesis account Adam not only gave in but attempted to justify his behavior by saying, "The woman tempted me and I did eat." Jesus makes plain that instead of (1) blaming someone else and (2) giving in to evil, we can (1) accept responsibility ourselves and (2) eventually learn to complete the sentence differently: "I was tempted but I was not persuaded; I resisted." It seems most likely that the account of the temptation of Jesus in Matthew is placed where it is, right after his baptism, to remind the Christian reader that battles and temptations do not end with baptism, with incorporation into the Lord.

Among other lessons, the story proclaims that even though we easily tend to believe that yes is the inevitable answer to evil, that everyone has a price, this is not so. The power of God is present in Jesus Christ, and through him in all those who are joined to him by faith. He is in us to overcome evil. He is not merely a picture of what might be or even of what will be, but of what is possible now. The conquest of evil has already begun in us and through us. It might be worth adding, too, that instead of complaining about the success of evil in our world, we are charged with working against it in his power.

To appreciate more what Jesus is to us, we need to emphasize a bit what Adam and Eve are to us. Their story, as we must have heard by now, is not primarily the recounting of a day in the life of an Australopithecus or Zinjanthropus couple who lived in a garden-like estate just north or south of the confluence of the Tigris and Euphrates. What's important about them is that they represent all of us: they express the author's conviction that the tendency of your basic human rascal is to self-seeking and lack of trust in God.

Another element in the background of this Gospel story is a third biblical temptation story, an account in Deuteronomy (chs. 6–8) of the trials and failures of God's people Israel on their way through the desert to the Promised Land. When they were tried and tested, they gave up on the Lord and turned to false gods, seeking help elsewhere. All of Jesus' responses to the devil in Matthew are taken from these same chapters in the Hebrew Scriptures. His quotations reverse the discouraging pattern of failure and lack of trust in God, the search for other, easier, and more showy solutions to our problems. And Jesus has passed his tests in the desert not simply to his own credit but for us. The New Testament, especially St. Paul, tells us that even though there has been this pattern of sin and lack of faith, that has all been turned around by Jesus. The grace of Jesus is much more able to change us than the example of Adam was able to keep us chained. They are not equal forces.

No matter how disillusioning our friends, our family even, our politicians, our heroes, our leaders may be; no matter how many cheap deals and how much profiteering from death-dealing arms sales there may be; no matter how many power-mad and money-mad people we meet, how many racists and cheats; and no matter how much of this we see looking back at us in the mirror; in Jesus Christ we know that we can overcome.

His teaching assumes the fact of our responsibility and adds to that the promise that the strength to do good, to say no to evil, becomes real by faith and trust in him. At times, maybe most often, somewhat like the losing team, the Christian may have to come back again and again, always hoping, trusting, resolving on a better season. The cycles of human life and the liturgy offer us any number of appropriate reminders: January 1, the beginning of Lent or Advent, the Easter season—to put it very elementally, the liturgy really only tells us the same thing over and over again in different colored vestments—a new turn in our life such as a graduation, beginning a new job, moving, turning forty. We need not just one but many new beginnings.

It would be too simple to say that Jesus saves us or does all of this for us by paying off some debt of ours to a "teller in the Divine Savings and Loan Association" (Andrew Greeley's term). Nor does he force it upon us. Rather, he is the powerful beginning of a new trend away from evil, a beginning that we are made part of through baptism, the Eucharist, our faith in him, and our willingness to hope and trust. Christian belief is that, no matter how indiscernible it may be, his victory is already at work on the resistance of ourselves and our world.

To a great degree the sin of Adam and Eve was mistrust; the sin of the Israelites was lack of trust. Each new beginning for us must be an effort to revive our trust, to throw away our cynicism, skepticism, hopelessness, and misplaced trust and to renew our idealism and spiritual youth. We need the help of exhortation, communal efforts, an Advent or Lenten season, the example of the reckless and hopeful young, a good book, or a retreat to fire up the life of faith given us in baptism. We are joined to the one who has overcome evil and despair.

We cannot be content to remain slobs or snobs, rude or lewd, avaricious or malicious, grouchy or grumpy. Linked more closely to Jesus in faith and sacraments, we can be transformed. All the desired changes will not be accomplished by this Easter or this Christmas or the end of this year or by age fifty or even by the end of our life—we will have to trust him for what will always be lacking. We will always be, in Luther's phrase, both sinners and saved. If they do nothing else of a positive nature in our lives, our sins and failings keep us in constant awareness of our need for a Savior, our dependence on the grace of the Lord. We can, with the help of that same grace, resolve that we will never stop hoping or trusting in him who put such confidence in our response that he risked dying for us on a cross.

Anybody Home?

The loss of awe is the great block to insight; a return to reverence is the first prerequisite for a revival of wisdom, for the discovery of the world as an allusion to God.   —ABRAHAM HESCHEL

Late have I loved you, O Beauty so ancient and so new; late have I loved You! For behold You were within me, and I outside; and I sought You outside; and in my unloveliness fell upon those lovely things You had made. You were with me and I was not with You. I was kept from You by those things, yet had they not been in You, they would not have been at all. You did call and cry to me and break open my deafness. . . . I tasted You, and now hunger and thirst for You; You touched me, and now I burn for Your peace.   —ST. AUGUSTINE

Graces are divine gifts, independent of human merit, but dependent on the human readiness to receive them. And the readiness itself is the first gift of grace, which can be either preserved or lost.   —PAUL TILLICH

I don't know Who—or what—put the question. I don't know when it was put. I don't even remember answering. But at some moment I did answer Yes to Someone—or Something—and from that hour I was certain that existence is meaningful and that therefore, my life, in self-surrender, had a goal.   —DAG HAMMARSKJOLD

God spoke once and is now silent. So wrote the renowned philosopher Jean-Paul Sartre. Scripture tells us quite the opposite: God's call to us, his concern for us, is unrelenting. God continually speaks to us, approaches us. He even seeks us out, as Francis Thompson wrote, with "unhurrying chase with unperturbed pace." It is we who don't hear, who can't see, who are absent or hiding.

Typical of the Bible's recurring theme is the parable in Matthew 22:1-10 that likens God's call to us to a king's invitation to a wedding banquet for his son. One gets the impression that the wedding feast in question, a symbol of eternal fulfillment, is modeled on the proverbial country wedding. This one's been going on not simply for weeks but for millenia. When the invited guests offer excuses, the king tries again. And he who tells the parable, of course, is Jesus himself, come as man to stress dramatically the urgency of God's invitation. Knowing the snarls in our postal system, we can readily appreciate God's decision to send a personal representative rather than depending on the mail. And in a sense, he had tried the mail. He had sent the written message we call the Hebrew Scriptures or the Old Testament, and too many had treated it like junk mail, throwing it away unread.

If we go back to the first book of those Scriptures, Genesis, to the story of the first parents, we have the point made with delightful concreteness. There we have details too readily dismissed as simply a matter of giving God human characteristics. Adam and Eve had eaten the forbidden fruit and are hiding. God walks in the garden, enjoying the evening breeze, the writer tells us. In the light of the Gospel story of the wedding feast, his words to the pair take on universal meaning. He says to the invisible culprits: "Where are you?" Really, that's in many ways an adequate summation of much of Scripture: God is forever saying, "Adam, Eve, George, Sue, Debbie, John, Sally, Sheridan, where are you?" There is certainly some validity to speaking of our seeking God, but that presupposes the theme we are concerned with here: that God first seeks us.

In stressing this point, I do not intend to forget that many who read this do consider themselves, to varying degrees, believers. What is being urged is that there is room in the lives of all of us for *more attention, better hearing.* Answering God's continual call, "Where are you?" and "Come to the wedding feast," is not a once-for-all matter any more than the call is. The call can be heard and answered ever more clearly and generously.

Some ignored the king's invitation and some just went their own ways: to their farms, their businesses, their personal concerns. We ignore the invitation by being, in effect, preoccupied or self-enclosed, self-satisfied, prematurely sure that we know what we should see or hear. This is one reason why "seeking" must in many ways take a back seat to listening, seeing. The hero of Hermann Hesse's *Siddhartha* tells a long-questing and unsatisfied friend that too much seeking may result in an inability to find or absorb something greater than what we are seeking—something beyond our imagination but often right under our noses. Intense seeking often and easily implies a too-specific concept of what we think we should find. Our conscience and the demands of love, the intuitions that come to us in silence and reflection, the intentions that hearing Scripture arouses in us, are better guides than our notion of what we think we should find. To a great degree, it is more a matter of being found than finding.

Or we fail to see or hear because of our near-total absorption in our livelihood, our farming and business, any of our tin gods: study, prestige, getting-ahead, science or art, any limited goal. All these, in a sense, serve to jam God's broadcast to us. Like Adam, we all too consistently hide our spiritual nakedness by snatching any available fig leaf. And the voices of common sense, or our neighbor, all justify our being concerned about matters such as our livelihood. They all tell us: grace doesn't buy shoes; prayer is no substitute for ground beef, etc. *That* we hear *all* the time. And it is inarguable as far as it goes. But the Gospel is never given us just to confirm middle-class assumptions or taken-for-granted human practices, but to challenge them. It tells us that our narrow concerns can dry us up and deaden us to all but our petty preoccupations. Paradoxically, being open to God and his word makes possible a deeper understanding of ourselves. In hearing him, "we are revealed to ourselves," says Martin Buber.

Charles Darwin may unfortunately speak for many in some pathetic reflections he wrote in the winter of his life. He deplored the fact that he had lost any taste for music and art and, his autobiography shows, for God, too. His mind had become, in his words, simply a "machine for grinding general laws out of large collections of facts." Whole segments of his mind had atrophied, and as a result he felt even his moral character had suffered. If he were to relive his life, he wrote, he would have set aside time at least once a week for poetry and music. It seems clear that what Darwin is regretting is the same thing the Gospel urges us to avoid: a rendering of ourselves deaf and blind to the call and invitation of God that flames in the beauty of autumn, that is hidden in every lure to love, that lies in the needs of the poor, that comes in the words of the Gospel and in those rare moments of genuine silence.

As long as we live, there is the danger of hearing and seeing less and less. Bifocals and hearing-aids signalize our aging. Conversely, as ordinary sight and hearing fail, there is still the possibility that we can see and hear more of the things of God. With St. Paul and all the heroes of faith, we can become more ready to answer the question "Where are you?" with "Lord, here I am; what must I do?"

> Behold, I stand at the door and knock; if anyone hears my voice and opens the door, I will come in to him and eat with him, and he with me."
> Rev 3:20

Interior Decorating

The Eucharist is a common meal eaten by those who are united through Jesus in love for one another. The Eucharist is a ritual commitment to the possibility of unity in friendship among human beings.
—ANDREW GREELEY

The deeper a symbol is rooted in the realities of everyday life—eating and drinking, body and blood—the greater the multiplicity of meaning that it contains.   —*A New Catechism*

The sanctuary is not the place set aside for us to encounter God (whom we are unremittingly reminded to seek in our neighbor), but the sacred place where we draw aside momentarily to rediscover and refresh our faith that it is in serving our neighbor that we cleave to God.
—JAMES T. BURTCHAELL

The most significant change for Catholic Christians among many in the last twenty years has been a matter of rearranging the furniture— moving the altar away from the end wall and letting it stand free nearer the congregation with the priest facing them. Why it ever got stuck against that back wall in the first place is a long sad story. One of the oddities of church history is that those beautiful Romanesque and Gothic cathedrals of Europe are also such clear monuments to a diminished apprehension of salient facets of the Lord's Supper. Art, architecture, and liturgy do not *necessarily* work together. The great value of the change, though, was to stress that the altar is basically a dinner table, a place for a meal, where the Lord's Last Supper with his friends is re- called and repeated with a circle of new friends. In terms of its place in the building and the place of the Eucharist (Mass or Lord's Supper) in Christian practice, this table along with the cross, which is intrinsically linked to this meal, is plainly the center of the life of those who follow

Christ. But we may still ask, How did a table become so essential to the Gospel of Christ? Why the great fuss about a dinner table?

Why? Because love and friendship are the center of human life. All the pain, effort, and preparation we put into developing friends; the tears over relationships that especially drench turbulent adolescence; the anxieties about friends; the worry about whether so-and-so will call; why she hasn't written; why there was no follow-up after homecoming; how I will live through the pain of breaking up; the moods going from the peaks of gladness to the pits of sadness—all this that is so exhausting and so disturbing to the mundane routine of life. What's it all about? What does it mean?

The agony and ecstasy are there because we correctly see love and friendship as being at the heart of human life. Progress or failure in them is decisive for all of us. Success and accomplishment elsewhere are hollow if there is no personal warmth at the heart of our life. And the Eucharist, this meal we share at this table, is there to tell us, to confirm with the authority of Jesus, that nothing is more valuable, more crucial, than love and friends. Like any meal taken together, but in a much deeper way, the Mass is essentially a feast of friends. This supper tells us that all the risks and pains of love are worth it; the waiting and false starts are worth it; the breakups and failures are worth it.

A good parable about the proper estimate of friendship and love over against the other elements of human life is the Gospel story of the unappreciative guests invited to the supper. Remember how they offered a variety of excuses for not coming. To think that our business, our careers and property, our investments, are more important than loving communion with other people is to miss the point of the meal and to miss the point of life itself. It means settling for a life of solitary and quick snacks at a standup food bar in an airport as we fly between deals. When our business and other trivia like money, success, and just plain *things* become too dominant, we are refusing the invitation to be truly human. In allowing those *things* to dominate us we are becoming like them: inanimate, cold, manipulative and manipulated, mechanical. Personal relationships have the upper hand in the Gospels as in genuinely human lives; a wedding feast is not to be spurned. Elsewhere throughout Scripture the final days and the ultimate realization we are pointed to are described in terms of a feast prepared by the Lord where all people, rugby players and drum majorettes, contemplative nuns and steel workers, politicians and poets, even Arabs and Jews, will sit down together in peace.

In agreement with all this, Jesus asks us to take part in a meal or supper in his memory. Do this in memory of me, he says; as often as you eat this bread and drink this cup, you will show my death until I come again. Elsewhere (in Mark) he says: This is my body; this is my blood . . . to be poured out on behalf of many. The meal really commemorates his life, death, and resurrection; the death is singled out as the decisive event which gives the clearest picture of God's love for us. The table we've been speaking about is, of course, also an altar where the sacrifice of Christ's obedience and surrender to God leading to death is represented at every celebration of this supper. This present discussion merely touches this sacrificial aspect of the Lord's Supper.

Belief and trust in the power of the love celebrated at this supper binds us together as Christians, and every Mass renews and toasts that love. The high point of Jesus' time with his disciples was their meals together (Andrew Greeley); even when he reappeared after his resurrection, it was in several instances to eat with them on the shore of Galilee, for instance, and with the disciples on the road to Emmaus. We re-create and strengthen our union with him and with each other by sharing in his meal. Inevitably and necessarily the table isn't large enough for all of us to sit around it together, and the bread and wine we take are in only symbolic quantities. After all, it is not just another meal; it is *the* meal par excellence. Even granted the attenuation of some of the aspects of a meal and the ritualized character (which has its own justification and value), the point of the celebration is still there: as we eat together we are rejoicing in and recalling the closeness of Jesus to us, and in him our closeness to God and each other. True, we'll never know some of those who attend with us; others we'll know but only as prickly annoyances. Human relationships *are not* what they should be. The further point persists: love and friendship are possible, and a goal as remote as the peaceful coexistence of all peoples—Democrats and dog lovers, musicians and musclemen—is worth working for and is intended by God.

Taking meals together is something we do so often and should prize so much more than we do. Even the most ordinary meal together— and it can get pretty darn ordinary in the cafeterias of our prepackaged and plastic age—even that signifies a willingness to be friends. Sitting down with someone else at a table shows a basic trust, can be an opportunity to widen our acquaintanceship and show some willingness to know others better.

The exceptional quality of the Lord's Supper, among others, is that it is a meal where the quantity of food and drink is minimal, but the power to increase love is at a maximum. It is the sign and constant reminder that genuine love, friendship, even lasting marriages, are possible in a world so full of enmity, unfaithfulness, suspicion, fear, and self-aggrandizement.

Assisting at the Eucharist should be a statement of faith and trust that our longing for total understanding and communion, for love and friendship—despite all the accompanying frustrations and failures, all the tears and fears—is ultimately important and realizable because God himself, who is love, is for it, is behind it. The only final failure would be to put other lesser matters before love or to despair of love.

A dinner table, the altar, odd as it seems, is at the center of the Christian religion because the love and fellowship it signifies are at the center of human life and human hopes.

Graduation Requirements

Love, like reason, is one of the elements of our knowledge.
—GEORGES BERNANOS

In spite of our boasted vigor we wait for the next age to be brought to us by Madison Avenue and General Motors. We do not prepare to go there by means of the good inner life. We wait, and in the meantime it slowly becomes easier to mistake longer cars or brighter lights for progress.
—LOREN EISELEY

Wisdom is a harmony of knowledge, will and feeling, and by no means necessarily grows with the growth of knowledge.   —BERTRAND RUSSELL

There is only one way to wisdom: awe. Forfeit your sense of awe, let your conceit diminish your ability to revere, and the universe becomes a marketplace for you.   —ABRAHAM HESCHEL

We're all sophomores, whatever our age or occupation. The suspected derivation of that word is from two Greek words meaning wise and foolish. Somewhere in history, second-year college and high-school students were pinned with that label, possibly referring to that mixture of growth, a dangerous *little* bit of knowledge and ignorance which observers have attributed to them more than to the rest of us. Nevertheless, that mix is shared by freshmen and seniors, faculty members as well: in fact, by all of us.

In the Gospel parable of the wise and foolish virgins (Matt 25:1-13), we have the two words illustrated. That story is concerned with the most dangerous kind of foolishness. (We shouldn't stretch the term too far and end up puritanically wagging our fingers at the high jinks of youth or the ebullience of people enjoying each other's company. Even, say, on the spur of the moment to invite the whole office staff home

67

for dinner might be foolish and inconvenient but not terminally foolish.) The virgins of the story are *dangerously* foolish; they are unprepared for the coming of the Lord, for their encounter with him. Wisdom is illustrated by the wise virgins, ready, prepared for life and death. Wisdom needs to be distinguished from an apparent facsimile, what we usually call knowledge. For the virgins to know the phone number of the nearest shop selling lamp oil would be knowledge, not wisdom. For many, in both the East and the West, who have reflected on the subject, knowledge—as ordinarily understood—is a kind of foolishness relative to wisdom.

Wisdom is meant to sound a bit lofty; it expresses one of those ideals we need if human life isn't to sink to a cynical, swinish, or merely trivial level. Where would human life be—where is it?—if we allowed another lofty term like love, for example, to be reduced to a transaction in a massage parlor? Ideals like wisdom, love, or faithfulness are ultimately more necessary to human life than good garbage disposal, city planning, foolproof national defense, and functioning zippers. Without ideals, human life can drop to a level as interesting and nourishing as a steady diet of snack food and hot dogs.

Knowledge, necessary as it is for the everyday conduct of human affairs, is not wisdom. Knowledge can mean being well informed about when income tax forms must be returned, having an understanding of when sheep will mate, or having comprehended something more arcane, such as the exponential decay curve of a discharging AC capacitor. That kind of knowledge is available to anyone with the required intelligence or some help from a book or a teacher. Knowledge can tell us how much stress a machine belt will take, how to harvest garlic without ruining our social life, how Beethoven structured his symphonies, and whether orbiting the planets is bad for our blood pressure. Wisdom, on the contrary, answers questions like: How should one deal with evil? What do we do about envy? What is the meaning of honesty? How do I face loneliness? Why does anyone need human society? How is real joy different from mere excitement? How do we justify the music of Beethoven? How do I help a friend? Why orbit the planets at all?

Knowledge is accessible to anyone: cheat, pimp, or pusher. Understanding relations between the Russian Empire and the Poles in the eighteenth century is unconnected with whether one beats his wife or not. A self-centered slob can learn the formula for pyrophosphoric acid as well as the most generous person can. Ordinary knowledge or a high I.Q. is independent of whether or not one is loving, just, or honest.

The attainment of wisdom, however, is possible only for those who love it, revere it, and seek it, who face the world and life with some reverence and willingness to be taught. The Book of Wisdom (6:12-16) personifies wisdom as a she, not just arbitrarily, and says of the quest for her:

> Wisdom is radiant and unfading, and she is easily discerned by those who love her, and is found by those who seek her. She hastens to make herself known to those who desire her. He who rises early to seek her will have no difficulty, for he will find her sitting at his gates. To fix one's thoughts on her is perfect understanding, and he who is vigilant on her account will soon be free from care, because she goes about seeking those worthy of her, and she graciously appears to them in their paths, and meets them in every thought.

Finding wisdom requires sensitivity of conscience, sincerity of intention. Wisdom comes to us only if we know our need, are patient, seek goodness, and recognize our foolishness. To the extent that we face ordinary life with reverence and respect she comes to us: "She graciously appears to them in their paths." We speak of mastering a body of knowledge but we do not master another person—except by perverting human relationships—nor do we conquer wisdom. The very posture is inimical to her meaning. We can transfer information orally or in print, but each must deserve, earn, grow into wisdom.

Wisdom is concerned with how to live rather than with how to make something, with how to appreciate rather than how to use. Wisdom is concerned with having and preserving friends rather than with making useful "contacts"; wisdom wants to know what is truly serious rather than what is merely profitable. Wisdom is more concerned with *being* than with *having*, more concerned with honesty than with getting ahead. Wisdom tends to marvel rather than to measure, to wonder rather than to weigh. Knowledge makes it possible for humans to build a 747, but without wisdom we will never get beyond the equivalent of Las Vegas.

Unless our necessary pursuit of knowledge is accompanied by some maturing in wisdom, we are in danger of seeing the world only as a marketplace (as Heschel says) or a toolbox or possibly just an adult sandbox. Wisdom tells us that looking for the immediately satisfying, the obviously profitable, the simply practical, is nearsighted and in the long run leaves us empty. Like the foolish maidens in the Gospel, without wisdom we will not be ready for death or life. We are truly foolish if we leave the search for wisdom to the last minute, to the unpromised years when we're too old to chase after bucks, sex, and kicks. We shouldn't be fearful or hesitant about offering the generous and idealistic young the challenge of something as exalted as wisdom or, in fact, of encouraging the typically youthful passion for something more than comfort and security. For them to settle for immediate and paltry goods alone, for a cushy position, is to age prematurely, to have as much verve, guts, and charm as a disgruntled old Scrooge.

I've spoken of wisdom as "she" or "her" after the example of the Book of Wisdom. That is because wisdom is a person to whom we can be attracted, whom we can love, and by whom we can be influenced. The New Testament rounds out the Book of Wisdom's view by telling us that wisdom became a human being like ourselves—Jesus Christ. He, St. Paul tells us, is the wisdom of God given to and for us.

As our wisdom, Christ alone gives us sure guidance in the direction of our lives. We learn or acquire wisdom only by saturating ourselves more and more in the words and life of Jesus. He is with us and available to us in his word, in our reflection on it, in prayer, in his body and blood, in work, in the life of the community of believers. He becomes our own wisdom when we decide to let ourselves be joined to him consciously, intelligently, and wholeheartedly.

Certainly, even after an adult commitment to him, we remain sophomores, a mixture of wisdom and foolishness. But, to the degree that Jesus Christ becomes the center and spur of our lives, we pass from that foggy state to a condition of wise readiness. We become "juniors," that much more ready for graduation, ready not simply for death but for life.

More than Commandments

To be a good loser seems at first sight a pathetic ideal. . . . Someone, as often as not, has to back off, and the Christian faith enables those who hold it to back off without feeling that their integrity and self-image are irreparably fractured, or that some loss of public esteem makes their future existence intolerable.   —JOHN F. X. HARRIOTT

I think there are far too many who count up how many times they attend Mass and rely almost entirely upon this for their salvation. They are convinced that they owe nothing further to Christ. Leaving church they immediately return to their former habits. I certainly do not hesitate to praise them for getting to Mass, but I am forced to condemn them for stopping at this point.   —ERASMUS

A Christian . . . is distinguished from someone who really is not a Christian, either reflexively or anonymously, by the fact that he does not turn his existence into a system, but rather allows himself without hesitation to be led through the multiplicity of reality, a reality which is also dark and obscure and incomprehensible.   —KARL RAHNER

Winning Through Intimidation is the title of one of the many "how-to" books that pander to our worship of success. The title expresses well the philosophy. Whether written by psychologists, businessmen, or TV preachers, they assert a view of life diametrically opposed to that of the one who won through the cross. His "how-to" book may well be the teaching found in chapters 5–7 of St. Matthew's Gospel, the Sermon on the Mount.

What is said there is enough to make all of us throw in the towel. Jesus puts before us a raft of seemingly impossible and unnatural goals. "How blest are those of a gentle spirit . . . those who show mercy . . . those who have suffered persecution. . . . Do not set yourself against the man who wrongs you. . . . Do not store up for yourselves treasures on earth. . . ." And much more in the same vein.

On one occasion when part of this text appears as the Sunday Gospel, the first reading illustrates it by a picture of King David exercising mercy toward his foe and pursuer King Saul. To use David as an illustration is more apt than first appears because, as with all of us, his mercy is coupled with much less charming characteristics. He is the same David who puts Bathsheba's husband on the line of death in battle in order to take her for himself—murder to cover up adultery. But any other example would have offered the same difficulties. Like David, we are all spiritual schizophrenics, torn between retaliation and forgiveness, aggressive self-assertion and gentle yielding, giving and gouging.

Yet, whatever the problem, there is no way to get around the teaching of the Sermon on the Mount. The words are not a collection of exaggerated, purposely shocking demands. They are essential to Jesus' teaching that love is higher than any law, including the laws of religion; they are the verbal counterpart to his suffering and death on the cross. The precepts in this discourse are not a sort of "honors course for those who have passed the Ten Commandments." They are for any and every one of his followers.

By attempting to follow them, we are imitating the mercy God has shown to us. In this, Jesus says, "you must be perfect," there must be no limit to your mercy (Matt 5:48). Throughout Scripture God's primary characteristic—and most consistent—is just this loving forgiveness, not his power or omniscience. His power we are all too ready to pretend to imitate; imitating God in that sense is at least as old as Genesis. In the mind of Jesus, however, we do nothing more gracious and generous than to imitate God's forgiving love toward us in regard to each other.

The world around us constantly urges us to walk an extra mile in the opposite direction: to think only of our rights, justice, our due, not letting people walk all over us. An ad for the book referred to in the opening lines of this essay reads:

> Before you "suit up" for your next "game" in the business world jungle, there are two realities you should face up to: "The results a person obtains are inversely proportionate to the degree to which he is intimidated. It's *not what* you say or do that counts, but what your posture is when you say or do it."

From the context it's clear that the "posture" must be one of aggressiveness and intimidation. With such help we come to think and speak of our more outrageous appetites as our due. And we easily think of vengeance. Even when we claim to be attempting to follow the other teachings of Jesus, we draw the line at "being taken," being gulled; the "manly" thing is always to be, as we say, one step ahead of one's competitors or adversaries. Like a character in a novel of Saul Bellow's who feels deeply offended, we've often thought: "I don't want to hurt the so-and-so; all I want is justice." And, often enough, that means as Bellow goes on to explain: "Justice! He wanted the fellow's guts in a shopping bag."

How do we take seriously such plain and painful teaching as that we should love those who curse us, give our shirt when our coat's already been taken, lend to and love those from whom we can really expect no repayment, and refrain from judging? At the very least such invitations must make us question, reappraise, the institutions and practices we live with and take for granted in everything from our economic system to our manner of education. If these admonitions represent God's judgment, then to withdraw some area of human life from their evaluation is to commit idolatry.

We know, of course, that judgment, courts of law, and power all have their place in the fabric of life. We must and do judge in many matters: in politics, in the classroom, in raising our children, in appraising a car or a car dealer. And none of us really believes in standing by passively in the face of great cruelty and flagrant abuse and saying: "Who am I to judge?" Correctly, we judge exploitation and cruelty as such and, God grant, try to stop them.

When and how, then, do we take Jesus' words seriously?

The words are meant—designed—to preclude any easy answer, to counter the efforts of religion at times, or at least of religious legalism, to reduce God's claim on us and human life to a set of rules and practices. Ultimately there can be no answer except the response of our own conscience to such demands, a response in the degree and manner we can here and now achieve.

Elise Boulding, a Quaker writer, has written *Born Remembering*, a booklet touching this. She describes how while on retreat she was deeply affected by Gandhi's teaching about "not wanting what the least of my brothers and sisters could not have." She says, "I wrote long letters home to the family about stripping ourselves of what we did not need." Their reaction and her own difficulty with this led her to conclude that *readiness* for such stripping or a call to free oneself of many things is a very individual and personal matter. All of us must recognize the Sermon on the Mount as a call to ideals we can grow into only in varying degrees with reflection, prayer, and exercise. Ultimately they will always ask more than we can achieve. In this way they throw us back on the *most Christian* of virtues, faith, and trust that God saves us, not we ourselves. But that trust does not simply free us from the need to pray and work to grow into the Sermon on the Mount.

No one can really tell anyone else exactly how to do it. Among other factors, our relation to other people, our responsibilities to them, all enter into the response we make at a particular moment to the limitless ideals of the Sermon on the Mount. The nature of its teaching is such as to leave all of us gasping and aware that there is always more we could do in the way of love, that love calls us to more rarefied surroundings. "Not to be taken advantage of" can never be the Christian's absolute. A Christian conscience, the Sermon on the Mount really says, has no office hours and no retirement age.

While the human race includes, somehow, Hitler and Idi Amin and mass murderers, we know too that it can include a St. Francis of Assisi and a Mahatma Gandhi. Like these latter and to our own degree, we are called to disarm the world, not by answering it in kind but by meeting its meanness with generosity. The Christian is to introduce into its mass a leaven that softens and bends human rigidity and harshness. The words of Jesus must prick us and leave us constantly unsatisfied. They demand that we question continually our own judgments and their absoluteness whether in business, in criminal justice, in politics and personal dispute, in academic and athletic areas of life, and even, through our participation in government, in disputes over borders and fishing rights.

The words of the Sermon on the Mount, with their call to limitless and indiscriminate giving, force us to ask: Is a new evil, a tit for tat, the best response to an evil? Is another gun the best answer to someone else's gun?

Only Seven?

For the church neither is nor wants to be anything else but the presence of Christ in time and space. —KARL RAHNER

They (sacraments) are mysteries because they embody the mysterious presence of God active in human situations and are the signs of it.
—J. D. CRICHTON

In fact, worship is an interlude in the actual business of salvation. . . . Yet this interlude is a most necessary one. It is the pause we need to glimpse the inwardness and the purpose and the eternal worth of what we do when we work. —JAMES T. BURTCHAELL

Henry James, Sr., father of the novelist of the same name and of the psychologist and philosopher William, instructed his daughter about his funeral. Tell the minister, he said, to say this: "Here lies a man who has thought all his life that the ceremonies attending birth, marriage, and death were all damned nonsense" (William Clebsch, *American Religious Thought*, 133). That remark must certainly resonate in the hearts of many an American brought up with the same ideal of undemonstrativeness and a kind of individualistic interiority. Besides that appeal, the words also reflect, I would hazard, the rationalism of this nineteenth-century New Englander or (since James had been involved quite a bit with the mystical Swedenborgians) a belief that religion was essentially very spiritual, that is, independent of the material in human nature.

The would-be rational person often finds the more instinctive and emotional aspects of human relations difficult to situate and embarrassing to face, as in ritual. Hence, the preference for lumping together religious rituals and actions the world over and labeling them superstitious, magical, or "damned nonsense." So often what our reason cannot express or categorize is left aside as irrelevant. Or if the ceremonies of religion are not discarded for reasons of reason, they are regarded as a concession to pictorial minds or naive materialists. These cannot be expected to perceive that God is spirit and—misunderstanding a text from John's Gospel—must be worshiped in spirit and truth, that is, without material or sensible accompaniments, within the mind and heart.

Within Christianity a strand of Reformation thought which was suspicious of what we would call the sacramental (the rites and ceremonies James was talking about) developed into the movement called Quakerism. George Fox, the saintly and ingenuous founder of the movement, felt it his mission to call people out of what he called "steeple-houses," that is, churches, to interior religion. The abiding result in Quaker practice was the rejection of all the sacraments. Rather than dilute the strongly held belief that God was present always and everywhere by celebrating that presence in some particular instance, the Quakers jettisoned the sacramental completely. As seems to be generally true, most of us are more balanced, more realistic in practice than our beliefs would often suggest. A few years ago I heard a well-known Quaker tell of how she took up the custom of praying the Hours (the breviary used by Catholic priests and religious which contains prayers for particular moments of the day). Without some such pinpointing, she came to believe, the generalized presence of God tended to evaporate, became as unsubstantial as the scent of last summer's roses.

One can presume without having to produce statistical data that Quaker boys have in the past squeezed Quaker girls and probably still do and that our most intellectual and spiritual friends, barring some psychological disability, do kiss their wives and children. None of us lives long without some such nonverbal communication with others. And we all depend on constantly renewed communication, at the very least by letter, to keep alive relationships with persons far removed from us by circumstances. If they are out of sight and we are out of mail, visits, and phone calls for too long, eventually they are also out of mind and we are out of what might have been love or friendship.

Obviously, cultural factors influence the way in which we express ourselves. There may be good reasons, it seems to me, to allow Scots and Laplanders to express their religion differently than Sicilians. One of the happy results of the spirit unleashed by the Second Vatican Council seems to be more recognition of cultural differences, of the need to allow for African and American liturgies, for instance, that give shape to God's presence differently than was done in sixth-century Rome.

Despite Henry James' strictures, the question is not whether we will use rites and ceremonies, but what kind they will be and how we understand them. Even James' vitriolic remarks were made with the assumption that there would be a funeral, that is, an ancient rite performed on the occasion of a death. How, then, do we understand these rites called sacraments and sacramentals in Catholic teaching?

Implicit already in this essay is a notion of a sacrament or the sacramental which will be developed further in the pages that follow. Most basic to the notion, in my understanding and reflection, is the conviction that the presence and love of God need to be made concrete, particular, tied to something specific, for beings who operate as we do on various levels including very much that of the senses. Sacraments are ways of focusing God's presence in our lives at particular moments and places; they celebrate his concern and attendance at birth and in the various passages of life—entering adulthood, marriage, illness, death—and in the more ordinary and daily events of human life such as eating and drinking with others. This does not exhaust the theology of sacraments by any means but it is one indispensable perspective on them. Along with many of the world's religions, Christianity has a strong conviction that God is omnipresent; equally strong is the belief that we experience that presence along with his power and love at key moments. Again, this matter seems somewhat paralleled in other religions too, especially, say, popular Hinduism with its many rites, holy places, and holy people.

Most distinctive to Christianity, it seems, is the central belief of the Christian that God has confirmed his presence and involvement in our world in a dramatic and unique manner which we call the incarnation. In a way similar to that in which we are to realize God is present in John Kozloski this July 3, 1982, at the corner of Laurel and Davis Streets in Dubuque, God became man (we say in the Creed) in Palestine at the beginning of our era as Jesus, son of Mary and Joseph. In a unique, historical way, he came to confirm that God is accessible at all times and in every place. In all this, Christianity and the God of the New Testament are in continuity with what Old Testament believers held. Reading the Old Testament, one is continually amazed by the effort made by the Jews to see God in everything that happened to them, including a takeover by the Assyrians. There he is perceived as the justly chastising father; in victory and prosperity his benevolent love is obvious.

As I see it, the Lord constantly reminded those who believed in him in the Old Testament that his love was faithful, enduring, even able to survive death, and all this was dramatically and finally confirmed when he entered human life in a genuine human existence and endured even the results of rejection—suffering and death on a cross. No human being has ever had greater love than this for us. God, in the person of this man Jesus, his Son, goes through our death—itself an adequate picture of his love for us—and then raises him up beyond death to everlasting life with himself. His love is here *with us* in a most gruesome death and, beyond that, he assures us we are with him without end.

All this is, in a sense, God's intervention to clarify something which is not all that clear in nature and the world's events. Invitations to see God in the beauty of sunset and sunrise, in the power of the sea, in the beauty of a flower or of a human smile, have value so long as we do not have to advert to the terrible destruction which winds and rains can wreak or to the ravages of cancer or to the seemingly demonic cruelty of which our race is capable. Nature and the observable world are at best ambiguous reminders of God's presence and love. Our fellow travelers on the planet can be sacraments of God's love with varying degrees of transparency—or visible signs of the presence of something more than humanly cruel. To see God in our world requires a kind of minimal faith, an openness to the possibility that not only the ordinary but also the extraordinary can reveal him (that is, there are no miracles for me apart from faith), and an acceptance of Jesus as his revelation to us. The latter has already been touched on and requires some basic study; the requisite openness may need a few more words.

We are often tempted (any weaker word than that will not do) to believe that we require some more obvious signs than those we have; once we have them, faith will be inevitable and full. The basic message of Scripture is all against that, no matter how many fast-buck evangelists tick off the signs. When the rich man in hell wanted someone raised from the dead to drop by at his brothers' homes and warn them, the response of Jesus was disappointingly mundane: if they have not listened, do not listen, to Moses and the prophets—the Scriptures and the proclaimers of God's word—they will not be convinced even if one should rise from the dead. Jesus himself did not wake up the Pharisees during the early hours of Easter morn and ask them what they thought *now!* He appeared only to those who had shown him at least some stumbling and halting openness and receptivity. "There is no way of demonstrating spiritual truth to those whose minds and hearts are not open" (*Interpreters' Bible*).

The kingdom of God is here now, present now, at hand, even within; there is no point in waiting for some future when the signs will be clearer. There can never be clearer signs; there can only be clearer hearts and clearer eyes to see what is already here. God's willingness to be perceived is not in question; "only the beholder is wanting" (G. M. Hopkins). As one sees the parade of signs and wonders that so many look to for final clarity, and our gullibility when it comes to the opportunity (so-called) to have more stunning evidence for God's presence in the world, one cannot but reflect that if some complain about the lack of signs, no one can complain about the lack of suckers. No sign in the sky or elsewhere is needed; from the parables we know that Christ is poised always, everywhere, to enter any life that opens to him. Literally we have been bombarded from Moses to the microwave, from Hammurabi to Heathkit, with the message: the grace of God is within you, at hand. "Before you call upon me, I am here."

In one sense, indeed, we must expect to find God, to see or hear Christ, in the extraordinary, the unknown. But that is not in Kohoutek or the cataclysmic but in places and persons where we do not really want to find him: in the unpleasant and abrasive prophet, in the poor and desperate whose very existence rebukes our comfort. The extraordinary and unknown in which we are to see God's presence are those places and persons that do not correspond to our romantic vision of how God would appear. Chapter 25 of St. Matthew tells it: he is to be found and served in the hungry, the imprisoned, the thirsty, the naked, the sick, the stranger. We are not to look so much for him coming in the clouds, but today, now, in us clods. In Luke's account of the appearance of Christ to the disciples on the way to Emmaus, we have confirmed that he is to be discovered in the strange and unknown—they do not recognize him— and the very mundane, the food and drink of a daily meal. The two are not all that separate; they merge in him. With our temptations to seek God in the flamboyant and fantastic, seeing him in the ordinary may be, after all, a formidable task.

The common and the familiar are very much the milieu of the sacraments. Water, food and drink, oil (the cure-all and all-purpose liniment of the ancients) are but particular instances, hallowed by an awesome and not negligible tradition, of how the world of such humdrum elements can be the channel of the life and presence of God. Through the age-old words of Scripture and the Gospels, the words and actions of our fellow humans, we can be assured as often as necessary of the basic worth of living, of the value in the struggle, of the concern of Someone of surpassing capability about our ills, problems, and failures. Putting off seeing God where he is excuses us and prevents us from living wholeheartedly here and now, gives us alibis for holding back on a commitment and for postponing real life. "Does the fish soar to find the ocean, the eagle plunge to find the air?" (Thompson). No, but we put off our own conversion and our happiness by looking everywhere but to the given and familiar—the Gospels, our neighbors, our own hearts—for the kingdom, the presence and power of Jesus.

Clearly, and contrary to some of our past spirituality, it seems necessary to admit, the sacraments are not momentary and mystical escapes from the real world into the world of magic and abracadabra. Rather, the sacraments push us to discern and see God in the most mundane, ordinary, usual events, things, and persons of our lives. By spotlighting the activity and love of God in specific moments, places, and things of ordinary life, the sacraments urge us to see all of creation and history as capable of unveiling God to the believer. The necessary prerequisite is our faith—or, put more broadly—our openness, our willingness to hear and see. That can hardly be overstated. Nothing can replace that condition: we do not have a God who is going to bludgeon us into believing in him or seeing his activity in the world.

It might be good to point out here that this basic receptivity, this precondition for God's activity in us, his unveiling of himself to us, is also necessarily operative in the far more basic matter of our apprehension of his existence. So often our problems about the existence of God are built up around an implicit rebuke of God for not being more patent, as if, to use the title of a C. S. Lewis book, he were in the dock and had to answer a series of complaints. More often, as Martin Buber says, "the eclipse of God" results from our placing something between ourselves and him, not vice versa.

> The angels keep their ancient places—
> Turn but a stone, and start a wing!
> Tis you, tis your estranged faces
> That miss the many-splendoured thing.
>
> Francis Thompson

The human being's ability to recognize in any minimal way not simply God's presence in the word but his very reality depends on openness, on an opening of a door that can be unlatched only from within.

Over the centuries the church has signalized seven particular moments of human life as sacraments. Presuming we recognize the church as embodying the voice of the community's tradition, these seven sacraments demand a special place in the life of the Catholic, though within the seven, they will be of varying importance to individuals. Some, like baptism and the Eucharist, are the pivots of Christian religion and are rooted in injunctions of the Lord himself: Do this in memory of me. To see the seven as *the* sacred moments when we meet God and are empowered by him as a community and individually should not prevent us from seeing his presence and power in many other junctures of human life in, possibly, some more personal and individualized "sacraments." Traditionally even the number of sacraments practiced by the church has varied till the sacred number of seven was finally settled on. If they are to signalize God's presence in human life, focus his power and help at both crucial and common times, what is there to prevent us from seeing and celebrating God's presence and power in many other times and places?

Taking Self Lightly

It is the test of a good religion whether you can joke about it.
—G. K. CHESTERTON

The profoundest definition of homo sapiens may be that which describes him as "the animal who laughs." Isn't it a certain preoccupation with other people's attitudes to ourselves that most of all puts a damper upon humor? Detachment is the secret; free from personal egoism we can see the world in its right perspective. Lacking a sense of humor is a clear imperfection in a human being. —L. MENZIES

An event becomes humorous when it is taken out of its limited frame and placed in a larger one. —SENGAI

(Of a man he apparently did not admire:) A solemn, unsmiling, sanctimonious old iceberg that looks like he was waiting for a vacancy in the Trinity. —MARK TWAIN

We should consider every day lost on which we have not danced at least once. And we should call every truth false which was not accompanied by at least one laugh. —FRIEDRICH NIETZSCHE

When a man promises himself suicide as a sort of reward we can be certain that matters have come near to their nadir. At the beginning of *Steppenwolf,* Hermann Hesse's novel, the "hero," Harry Haller, has made just such a compact with himself; he is out of step with the world around him and exasperated with it and with himself. Much of the story revolves around the efforts of several acquaintances and friends to advise remedies for Harry short of arsenic or a leap from the nearest bridge. One suggestion made is that he look at life less ponderously, with some sense of humor about himself. Such humor, the author says, "is perhaps the most inborn and brilliant achievement of the human spirit." How "inborn" it is may be questionable; that it is an "achievement" seems better attested by its frequent absence. In many areas of life—in the world of economic competition and business, of academia, of religion—there is a temptation for the more earnest among us to raise everything to a dreadfully serious level, to view every episode and event as of life-and-death importance. Each tends to regard his or her work as the most important project to hit the planet since the building of the ark or the discovery of aspirin. Such an atmosphere produces the tediously business-like, tightly coiled, no-guff types who are beyond small talk and matters of mere humanity.

Our adult world is full of such wooden gravity and self-importance. Humor is tolerated as a diversion for the light-minded, those not really concerned about "getting ahead," or as recreation. (The latter, unfortunately for so many, comes down to watching television where, despite appearances, we are diverted not so much with humor as with a trivialization of reality.) In our so-called mature world everyone has a long list of things which are just not funny.

Undeniably, for the truly tragic moments of life the only decent response is seriousness, prayer, even sorrow and tears. Injustice, cruelty, greed, constant incompetence: all may call for anger, denunciation, serious action, even an occasional scream. The loss of someone close, illness, and disaster: these are hardly to be taken lightly, despite our hope in Christ or the consolation of others.

Granted all that, there remain many situations in life that are not truly dire, no matter how disturbing or irritating they may be. Even apart from the good of those around us, always a prime consideration when weighing the effect of our moods, our own happiness and health would benefit if we could find a better response than grouchiness, sadness, bitterness, or just excessive solemnity. Not everything that happens is worthy of being made into a Bergman film; some of life's moments are better seen as slapstick.

On the face of it Scripture seems to have little to say about humor and evidences minimal utilization of it. Laughter is mentioned in the Old Testament in connection with gloating over the ills of an enemy or taunting a foe. Yet the First Commandment, with its strictures against other gods, against giving anything in creation the unqualified importance and seriousness of God himself, certainly gets to the heart of what is meant here by a sense of humor about one's self and life. Not to make stocks and bonds, one's political party and opinions, one's possessions or position, one's athletic team or one's country, above all, one's self, so absolute that they rival God, that they cannot be questioned or criticized—that is the negative fulfillment of the First Commandment.

At least two passages in the Gospels and much of the tenor of the New Testament support the idea that our thought and actions are not all that momentous: Christ's words about becoming like children and his injunction to learn from the birds of the air and the flowers of the field. Whatever else it may mean to become like a child, it certainly seems to include a lack of self-conscious dignity and pomposity. To live like the birds and the flowers of the field (in its context) is to be reminded of the relativity of our control of affairs and ambitions. Jesus there urges a trust that frees us from worrying about what will happen if we loosen our grip on the world for a moment, and he gives us an assurance that even without our straining the sun will still rise. Mercifully he mitigates the serious prophetic spirit of much of Scripture with words about children, flowers, and birds.

Are not many problems handled better by some lightness? The inevitable discord between individuals: between parents and children (who have ever avoided being a real pain to their teenager?), between husband and wife, between roommates, between people using the same facilities. Or the failure of our pet projects, the embarrassment we suffer in personal matters. All these come off better, retain their proportion in our lives, if we can laugh them off, or laugh at ourselves and go on living. The lesser contradictions of life, those probably not worthy of being subsumed under the grandiose heading of "the problem of evil," leave us with no other alternative, short of a perpetual petulance, than to suspect that God himself must have a sense of humor. Someone has suggested that the reason the angels can fly is that they take themselves so lightly; even leaving aside the whole matter of angels and wings, the point remains. An easy touch about less essential matters, especially about our own dignity and importance, might make our own trip through life a bit more like flying and less like plodding. If crying doesn't help in the case of spilled milk—in fact it only adds to the puddle—laughing may well dry it up completely.

Humor, of course, is most safely used in regard to one's own problems. Ordinarily others must be left to take their own difficulties seriously if they wish. Sensitivity is necessary before we tell another to laugh off a broken leg or a broken heart, before we attempt to tell others that their problems are peanuts. To attempt to lighten them requires subtlety and a prior intimacy and understanding if the effort is not to be obtrusive, condescending, or belittling.

Ultimately, then, some elements in life just cannot and should not be laughed away: someone else's misery, important commitments, obligations, promises, conscience. In fact, to treat any issue at all with some lightness makes sense only if there are matters we must regard as unequivocally serious. But the small things: why give them more importance than they deserve? And, above all, why give ourselves more importance than we deserve? If it isn't a geocentric universe, all the less is it really an egocentric one. There is enough genuine calamity in human life without turning every moment into a crisis or a cross. So many matters become serious only because we choose to consider them so. Our self-importance dictates that everyone must know that I am not to be trifled with, that my work is vital to the continuation of the universe, etc. We're so afraid of being regarded as airheads that we end up being blockheads.

The contrary practice of looking at much of life, at ourselves, with some lightness is close, it seems to me, to our Lord's invitation to follow him in losing our life, in forgetting ourselves, in order to really find or reveal our true self, given more by him than it is made by our worried efforts. In the novel quoted earlier, Hesse says that "humor begins when a man ceases to take himself seriously." If that is true humor, it is also very close to or identical with true selflessness, that losing of one's self that Jesus teaches. Everything considered, a higher state than taking one's self seriously may well be that of taking one's self lightly.

Preparing the Gifts

Talent must be opposed and counterbalanced by character, inspiration by discipline, facility by inhibitions. —HERMANN HESSE

The essential thing . . . , it seems, is that there be obedience, long continued obedience in some one direction. When this happens, something worthwhile always comes of it in the end, something which makes living worthwhile: virtue, for example, or art or music or dance or reason or spirituality—something that transfigures us, something subtly refined, or mad, or divine. —FRIEDRICH NIETZSCHE

Trying to be religious without fasting and denying oneself is, to use Robert Frost's analogy about free verse, like playing tennis without a net. —YVONNE GOULET

German novelist Hermann Hesse ordinarily expressed his beliefs about how life should be lived in his novels: *Siddhartha, Narcissus and Goldmund, Steppenwolf, The Glass Bead Game,* to name the major ones. Taken all together, his strongly didactic fiction offers a balanced vision of human spiritual development devised by one who had rejected the Lutheran Pietism of his youth in favor of his own wide-ranging search for wisdom about human life. Young people of the last couple of decades could and often did find much less trustworthy gurus than Hesse. In a few essays, Hesse approached some systematization of his thought. And in the letter quoted here, he attempted to reconcile two profound and divergent currents in the history of the human psyche.

The inmost urge of youth is to take oneself seriously; the drive of old age is towards being able to sacrifice oneself. . . . I do not like to formulate dogmas but my firm belief is that a spiritual life must develop and move between these two poles. The calling, the yearning, the duty of youth is development; the calling of maturity is to abandon and surrender oneself or, in the words of the German mystics, "to be no longer concerned with becoming." But unless we attain maturity and some true development of personality and unless the accompanying pains are endured, we will have nothing to offer when we are older.

trans. Knute Anderson, O.S.B., and Wilfred Theisen, O.S.B.

The two poles are familiar: development and self-sacrifice, or self-realization and self-forgetting. Very clearly the contemporary stress in psychology and educational theory, for example, has been on our becoming our real selves, on self-realization, unfolding our potential, etc. (The flood of paperback self-improvement or unlock-your-own-potential books is quite enough to drive even the most sympathetic reader to some nihilistic rejection of the whole enterprise.) Strong statements in the New Testament and a one-sided emphasis by Christian spirituality on self-sacrifice, self-denial, and self-effacement long ago produced the expectable reaction in Nietzsche's denunciation of Christianity's weak-kneed denial of life and his exaltation of the instinctual, the individual, and the generously virile. The books mentioned continue the protest in a watered-down, more genteel, manner; in fact, so genteel that the ordinary Christian seldom thinks of them as confronting any aspect of Christian teaching.

There is, of course, the paradoxical truth, hallowed in the New Testament, that by giving ourselves to someone or something beyond ourselves, we do discover our own best self: "He who loses himself for my sake will find himself" (Matt 10:39). That is very likely the last word, a word that transcends everyday human behavior and psychological models of human development. And, the idea of human maturity achieved by our efforts and by dint of planning, a rationally devised regimen, etc., may be quite illusory. Human maturity seems to be ultimately a gift, not an achievement, a prize more surely ours to the degree we cease to strive consciously for it. But, granted all that, no one lives a life devoid of purposeful self-development, education. Even St. John of the Cross must have deliberately worked at the rules of Spanish grammar and composition to write his compelling poems about the joys of self-forgetting. The Hindu *Upanishads* term the knowledge and skills which we learn and use in everyday life a lower kind of knowledge compared to the knowledge of one's ultimate identity with Brahman but, nevertheless, they do—and we must—term such development and effort a necessary type of knowledge.

So we are faced with two legitimate sets of counsel: develop yourself, realize yourself, unfold your potential; on the other hand, forget yourself, give yourself away, surrender. And they point decisively in opposite directions. Hesse and many others have not been content to leave them distinct, simply existing on parallel planes.

Hesse argues that the two propensities have their proper *time* in a person's life—the one in youth, the other in old age—but also that they must coexist throughout life. It seems best to think of them as forming a pattern or a rhythm in human life. We develop a power, we acquire a skill, we fulfill ourselves, only to be able to give something, to do something, and this happens again and again on different levels. The budding vocalist gets self-worth and gives pleasure by singing in the summer production of *Brigadoon*. The athletic skills that Olympic competitors learn in their teens can give others pleasure and excitement when they perform in their twenties, and they receive a sense of satisfaction themselves. Even the two-year-old likes to exhibit a new-found ability to pull the table cover off. "Lookit, Mama," cries the youngster in the swimming pool. Fortunately, we do not and we should not wait for old age to give of ourselves and our development. And, likewise, age should not mean that we cease growing and learning, even though it may be at a slower rate than in youth. The young may need patience to be willing to learn from the old and from experience and history, and the old often have to learn that how much one gives of one's memories and experience depends on the receptivity of the hearers or presumed beneficiaries.

To unfold, to blossom, to realize this or that talent and capacity in ourselves, is what we rightly expect in youth, in the years of fastest growth. The other tendency—to want to give, to use a power—while it may certainly be an act of selflessness sustained by grace, also has its natural foundation in an apparently spontaneous desire we all witness and share in daily. A woman skilled in higher mathematics finds it hard to be content with running an elevator, though this may easily be her fate in our strange economy. Even the student   envied wistfully by others for the gracious opportunity of just learning, absorbing, even contemplating— grows restless as a learner and itches to show how he or she would run the world or take responsibility. The ideal parent or teacher learns to provide opportunities for responsibility in the child or student and allows gradually more and more openings for decision and action.

A good human life requires a rhythm that allows place for both development and exercise, acquisition and giving away, self-realization and self-surrender. There is a danger in proposing as the exclusive task for the young self-sacrifice, self-denial, as the past seems to illustrate. There is a time—and that is in youth, primarily—when development, self-realization, should be encouraged to the extent that time and energy allow. The body and the mind, the heart and the reason, the private and the social: all deserve scope for some realization. Even the unthinking excesses of narcissistic attention to self-development cannot invalidate the need for time and place for some concentration on self and personal growth. Truly catholic Christianity should be notable for an acceptance of both tendencies and an unwillingness to sacrifice one to the other.

Self-development is not simply the consequence of some uninhibited adoration of self but seems to be of a piece with the idea of human stewardship of the gifts of creation. The raw materials of our existence and all of nature, including ourselves, deserve the attention and work needed to form them into something that further enhances life or serves to offer God worship. The transformation also satisfies our own need to create and exercise our powers. Furthermore, as mankind's rearing of the young generally attests, both the Father and our fellow humans deserve more than the crude material and spiritual endowments with which we were born. Our cooperation, ingenuity, and work turn the rough-hewn blocks of creation and evolution into monuments to intelligence, will, and feeling. To produce new wonders for eye, ear, touch, mind, and heart is the duty of any kind of art, including the art of living.

Once something has been developed, once a talent has matured, once an ability has been refined, there is something to offer in love, something to give, something to sacrifice, something to surrender to others and to God. The more we have become our best selves, the more there is to give. As if developing Hesse's theme, Teilhard de Chardin writes:

> There can be no sweet-smelling smoke without incense; no sacrifice without a victim. How would a man give himself to God if he did not fully exist? What possessions could he offer if his hands were empty? . . . The question at stake is rather clumsily formulated at times as: Which is better for a Christian—passivity or activity? Development or renunciation? The general answer is: Why separate and contrast the two natural phases of one single effort? Our essential desire and duty is to be united to God. But in order to be united, we must first of all *be*—be ourselves as completely as possible. . . . Once this has been accomplished there is time to think about renunciation, giving oneself away.
> *The Divine Milieu* (New York: Harper & Row, 1960) 95–96.

Or, back to Hesse's words, "Unless we attain some true development and endure all the accompanying pains, self-discipline, there will be nothing to give, nothing to offer."

Stronger than Death

Christ did not die to save people, but to teach people how to save each other. This is, I have no doubt, a grave heresy, but it is also a fact.
—Oscar Wilde

It is only because the person whom I idealize actually exists that I can love the idealized one. . . . But does not the motive force which enables and empowers us to idealize a beloved person arise from the deepest substance of that beloved person? Is not the true idealization in the deepest sense a *discovery* of the essential self meant by God in creating the person whom I love?   —Martin Buber

We are, all of us, moulded and remoulded by those who have loved us, and though that love may pass, we remain none the less their work. . . . No love, no friendship ever crosses the path of our destiny without leaving some mark upon it forever.   —Francois Mauriac

Is it the beautiful, the eternal in things, which awakes and kindles our love for them, or is it our love for things which reveals to us the beautiful, the eternal, in them?   —Miguel Unamuno

I have met in my life two persons, one a man, the other a woman, who convinced me that they were persons of sanctity. Utterly different in character, upbringing and interests as they were, their effect on me was the same. In their presence I felt myself to be ten times as nice, ten times as intelligent, ten times as good-looking as I really am.   —W. H. Auden

In fifteenth-century France there lived a great poet about whom we know little except his reputation for brawling and friendship and his insight into the contradictions and brevity of all that is human. His name: François Villon. His poems have survived and many know his most famous line: "Where are the snows of yesteryear?" In other plaintive verses Villon wonders where all the friends of his youth are, the "happy young men, gifted in song and talk, graceful in word and deed." He muses with spare melancholy: "Some are stiff and dead; may they find rest in paradise."

Of the many people we have known and with whom we have shared the happiness and hazards, the bruises and beers, say, of college life or youth, how many do we still know or remember after a decade or two? Maybe we do vaguely remember them but "know" them in the sense of continued, growing contact? Some, close for a few years of school, walk out of our lives with the graduation recessional. Our own love and capacities go only so far, and then some great smile, some ready, sensitive heart, some serious companion or love of our youth—when we seem most open to new friends—is crowded out by new personalities and interests. Forces beyond our control will and do take others. Even during youth we have the experience of friends swept away by untimely death in accidents or illness.

> Death or distance soon consumes them: wind
> > What most I may eye after, be in at the end
> I cannot, and out of sight is out of mind.

If there is any consolation or truth in the Christian faith, it must mean that we can entrust to the Father, to Christ, the people we ourselves cannot follow with our love and interest. God's love and concern are not limited like a warranty on a car, or by bifocals; if he counts every sparrow, the Gospel tells us, he certainly cares for us. His care goes around the corners our friends turn that take them out of our sight and lives. Gerard Manley Hopkins, in "The Lantern Out of Doors," quoted at the end of the previous paragraph, continues:

> Men go by me whom either beauty bright
> > In mould or mind or what not else makes rare:
> > They rain against our muck-thick and marsh air
> Rich beams, till death or distance buys them quite.

And though we can only stand helpless as they disappear:
> > Christ minds; Christ's interest, what to avow or amend
> > > There, eyes them, heart wants, care haunts, foot follows kind,
> > Their ransom, their rescue, and first, fast, last friend.

Much of the Scriptures are filled with the conviction of God's everlasting love for us. Even in the psalms, written we are told before any Jewish conviction of an afterlife had developed, there are constant assertions that God's love and care for the psalmist will never fail, that it even goes beyond death, that it is more enduring than that of a mother. In the most obvious Scriptural reference for the subject of love and friendship, the Song of Solomon, that collection of opulent love poems, we read that "love is stronger than death; . . . many waters cannot quench [the fire of] love" (8:6–7). The resurrection of Jesus, of course, is the great confirmation and illustration of the full truth of all this: God's love and care do not just see us to the cemetery but beyond.

And are we not warranted in crediting our own love for others with some of that same durability? The lines from the Song of Solomon already suggest that our loves, human love, friendship, need not be ephemeral and meaningless episodes, testimony to youthful imprudence, but something that shares the eternity and persistence of God's love. Even apart from the testimony of Scripture there is the conviction in many of us that love given is never lost but only transformed, only passed on as if in an endless chain. Think of the love received from parents and friends that has provided the example and spur to our own love for others. The energy of love seems never to be lost but only transformed, given in another form.

With the poets it is hard not to believe that the experience of love is here and now a beginning (a pledge) of eternity, of risen life, something never lost but always kept, if not in our weak memories, then in the memory and mind of God. A force that came from him to begin with and which, despite our casual and superficial use of it at times, cannot be lost or destroyed, which more than anything else tells us that being loved is not just a dream or a mirage.

The New Testament confirms this in telling us that the loving service we give to others (feeding, healing, comforting, etc.) is given to the Lord himself (Matt 25). Karl Rahner has pointed out that this is what justifies the absoluteness and unconditionality of love. This present essay is saying that the idealism—some would say the romanticism—of poets and lovers surrounds the same intuition arrived at, however, by means of the personal experience of love.

What limits love, kills it, or makes us think that it has disappeared or never existed is our shortsighted view that love is love only when there is a return, preferably a return of the same quality and force. But if genuine love is the transmission of something that comes ultimately from God, it must share some of the disinterestedness of God's own love, that love which loves us prior to our desirability or merit and creates good in us. Love on our part, of course, does involve attraction and desire —to attempt to rule them out would be to misunderstand the human—

but, further, it must share in this self-forgetfulness, freedom from concern about results and responses.

Freedom is possibly the key word. If love is not to be simply lustful grasping, it must have the character of freedom about it. Those who are loved must sense that they are not our possessions. To have loved must be itself our own reward. In giving love Christians can be sure that they are imitating God—in fact more than that, dispensing God's love to those in their own milieu. Freedom includes the willingness to let others be themselves, not just our appendages or reflections; it includes a willingness to let go. The most repeated example of this must be the necessity under which parents are of learning gradually to let their much-loved children become much-loved individuals, adults, with their own responsibility and their own lives, even with the right to make mistakes. Obviously, this freedom is two-sided: once parents have given their children good example and love, what cause can they have for berating themselves for every mistake or wrong turn taken by their growing children? Love will have its effects, we have every reason to believe and trust. We are not always guaranteed the additional pleasure of seeing the happy results.

All this, of course, suggests the character of the cross which is inherent in true love. Whether this is due to our desire to want things for ourselves, to exercise some of our primal idolatry and "would-be-like-God" desires, is another huge question. In any case, the notion of sacrifice or surrender or of letting go of what and whom we love is, for most of us, to some degree at least cause for pain, regret, even tears.

To sum up. We need confidence in the eternal value of any and all love we give, the conviction that it has its origin in God—when it shares to whatever degree in his selflessness and the non-grasping character of his love. We have reason to believe that our love will have effects, seen or not, of eternal resonance; that, even in the face of apparent rejection and recalcitrance, the power of love is the one true, inexorable power in the world. That it is a power stronger than death, a power that will ultimately rescue us all from the nothingness that otherwise seems to threaten.

We need, too, the confidence that God's love for our friends, as for ourselves, is more lasting and thorough than anything our most diligent care can imagine: something to be trusted, in which to let ourselves be carried.

Our conviction about the power and strength of God's love and the worth of our love is rooted in the all-permeating Christian conception that God ordinarily works through other human beings. As he spoke to and manifested his own love to us in the person of his word made flesh, the incarnation, his ordinary mode of action is the same. His grace, love, care, and concern come to us through other human hands, faces, smiles, words from parents to friends to wives and husbands.

Allied to this but going beyond it must be our conviction that while God will ordinarily work through us, he is not limited to that mode of operation. As he works outside the sacraments and church for and in those who have never heard his Gospel or who cannot bring themselves to accept it, so he works beyond what our actions, words, or love seem capable of doing. When the people on whom we have spent our love have disappeared, gone beyond our ken and concern, he is still with them as he is still with any of us in the desolation and pain that others cannot enter. His ways are *not simply* our ways, much as he may have chosen to use them. They are also much more than and different than our ways. To lock him into our patterns or expectations would be another kind of unfreedom. Here we touch another of the profound paradoxes that face us whenever we get more deeply into any element of the Christian faith.

Once more Gerard Manley Hopkins speaks to the issue. In "The Leaden Echo and the Golden Echo," a poem which begins with the human quest—"How to keep—how to keep beauty . . . from vanishing away?"—he speaks of God as the "place" where all we prize and love has its lasting home. Beauty is certainly a broad enough term to encompass all the good that we love and would preserve in others.

> I do know such a place
> Where whatever's prized and passes of us, everything that's fresh and
>   fast flying of us, seems to us sweet of us and swiftly away with,
>   done away with, undone. . . .
> The flower of beauty, fleece of beauty, too too apt to, ah! to fleet,
> Never fleets more, fastened with the tenderest truth
> To its own best being and its loveliness of youth; . . .
> . . . . the thing we freely forfeit is kept with fonder a care,
> Fonder a care kept than we could have kept it, kept
> Far with fonder a care (and we, we should have lost it) finer, fonder
> A care kept.

Too Good to Be True

Surely I haven't suffered simply that I, my crimes and my sufferings, may manure the soil of the future harmony for somebody else. I want to see with my own eyes the hind lie down with the lion and the victim rise up and embrace his murderer. I want to be there when every one suddenly understands what it has all been for. —F. DOSTOYEVSKY

But one has to see and recognize that life is threatened radically in order to grasp what God is and wants to be for us. It is only then that one can believe and hope and grasp God's promises in the good news of Jesus Christ. —KARL RAHNER

Atheists—What reason have they for saying that we cannot rise from the dead? What is more difficult, to be born or to rise again; that what has never been should be, or that what has been should be again? Is it more difficult to come into existence than to return to it? —BLAISE PASCAL

While shaving one morning in the Easter season to the accompaniment of the radio, I caught a phrase in the announcer's patter: "Anyone as nice as your true love must be hiding something." It reminded me of an old song: "You're just too good to be true." Both express rather lightly something like the doubt that the disciples express in Luke's Gospel when faced with the news of the resurrection. "They were still unconvinced, still wondering, for it seemed too good to be true" (24:41). In a very serious way we all share this tendency to distrust whatever seems perfect or, at least, much better than we expected. We tend to be suspicious of the man or woman who always does the correct thing and never says a rash or undignified word. Possibly we ordinary peons feel we have been manipulated and deceived too often by the powers that be, the politicians, corporations, etc. All this has the concomitant effect of making faith and trust more difficult. Like the disciples we are often hesitant about the most joyous and unique elements in Christ's life and teaching. Not only the risen appearances of Jesus but God's love for us, his presence with us—all seem too good to be true.

Whatever our excuses, this skepticism is, as the Gospel stories evidence, not new to our generation or our imagination. It is one of the stock objections of many nonbelievers to religion. Take, for example, a famous passage from Sigmund Freud:

> We tell ourselves that it would be very nice if there were a God who created the world and was a loving Father, and if there were a moral order in the universe and an afterlife; but it is a very striking fact that all this is exactly as we are bound to wish it to be. And it would be more remarkable still if our wretched, ignorant and downtrodden ancestors had succeeded in solving all these difficult riddles of the universe.
>
> *The Future of an Illusion,* ed. James Strachey and trans. W. D. Robson-Scott (Garden City, New York: Doubleday Anchor Books 1961) 52–53.

Freud's words about our "wretched, ignorant and down-trodden" ancestors sound quite condescending to us to whom technology daily shows its uglier side. We are ready once again to see some wisdom in those "wretched, ignorant and down-trodden" people. But the great psychoanalyst makes explicit a more basic and unjustified assumption by which we are all tempted: the assumption that the truth about reality, about life and afterlife, cannot be consoling; that it must be grim and bleak; that, somehow, hopelessness and despair are more noble than confidence and hope. (As someone has said, can you imagine Abraham Lincoln laughing?) It is the cynical view that what is glorious and beautiful and joyous cannot be true. But why? All of us are guilty of this same strange attitude; how often do we say that a book or movie is *realistic* when we really mean that it is brutal or sordid?

We are suspicious of the good and the gracious. The fellow who has been sighing over that beauty sitting near him in the office says, when she finally notices his existence, "I can't believe it; she spoke to me." Or we say, "I can't believe I got the job!" It's too good to be true.

Of course, it is more complicated than that. We react the same way to tragedies: "I can't believe it; he was here just yesterday." "Everything was going so beautifully, then this!" The truth may be that we are equally fearful of glorious excess and harrowing tragedy. As artists of one kind or another are always telling us: we prefer the safe, comfortable ground of the moderate even if it lacks all color or challenge. We prefer the bland to the blunt, the smug to the excessively provocative. But, for now, let us stay with our distrust of the good and the great.

In matters such as resurrection and God's will for us, part of the problem is that this timidity of ours attempts to limit God. In sending his Son to live, die, and rise again, he meant to expand our vision of what is possible, to break the bounds of what was thinkable. Thinkers over the ages have used their minds—legitimately—to speculate about God, but their conception of God as impassible, unalterable, above all human passion, unmoved, etc., noble as it is, must yield to what, in fact, God has done, to his revelation of himself in Jesus.

Lofty and consoling as all these matters are, our faith in them is ultimately much more important and *practical* than the ability to find a job, to repair a car, or even to be able to walk across the street by ourselves. Our faith that the Father does intend to raise us up on the last day, that his desire for us far surpasses any dreams we may have: this must be solidified, made part of our world view, made real by reflection, prayer, and our celebration of all this in the liturgy. Without the backdrop of this ultimate faith in God's amazing love for us, his faithfulness even beyond death, the difficult and terrible moments of life easily leave us embittered, peevish, sour. To be suspicious of or to refuse to accept the good God has determined for us can be a childish tantrum on our part, a refusal to accept what we have not thought of, a denial of the possibility of anything superior to ourselves or our ingenuity. Such an attitude is the opposite of that openness and capacity for wonder that is the irreducible supposition for any work of God in us and, also, for any impact of others on us. This churlishness is demonstrated more mundanely when we cut down another person's accomplishments out of pettiness and envy. In regard to God, the resurrection calls on us to acknowledge, despite Freud and friends, that the real problem with our wishful thinking, so-called, is that we can't wish far enough, that our dreams and wishes fall so short of the reality that radiates from Christ's resurrection.

To have and believe in this vision means that grace, beauty, love, joy, and eternal life are the final matters, not despair, pain, tragedy, sin. The world around us, above all the men and women who surround us, help assure us of this if, once again, we are open to their goodness. In them we can see grace, beauty, agility of mind and body, skills, vigor, gentleness, exuberance, a tremendous variety of talents in everything from music to the dance floor to the playing field to the hospital bed. All these are meant to be suggestions here and now of that renewed and perpetual youth and humankind that shines through the resurrection of Jesus.

Seeing the good and believing in the triumph of the joyous and beautiful will not preserve us from tears, disappointments, depression, or tragedy, but it will help us snap back from these inevitable periods because we'll know that these are not the last word. At times reality may seem to be made up entirely of pain, misery, and disaster—who would know better than he who hung on the cross?—but now he knows and we can know and trust through him that the last word God has for us is not one of discouragement and sadness (they were never his words at all) but of serenity and joy. For him nothing is too good to be true.

Our Pain and Our Pride

Even when one feels nearest to other people, something in one seems obstinately to belong to God and to refuse to enter into any earthly communion—at least that is how I should express it if I thought there was a God.   —BERTRAND RUSSELL

Isn't our aloneness largely removed in the encounter of the sexes? . . . The ecstasy of love can absorb one's own self in its union with the other self, and separation seems to be overcome. But after these moments, the isolation of self from self is felt even more deeply than before, sometimes even to the point of mutual repulsion. We have given too much of ourselves, and now we long to take back what was given. . . . Thus, man and woman remain alone even in the most intimate union. They cannot penetrate each other's innermost center. And if this were not so, they would not be helpers to each other; they could not have human community.
—PAUL TILLICH

A common practice is to avoid working up the courage required for authentic intimacy by shifting the issue to the body, making it a matter of simple physical courage. It is easier to be naked physically than to be naked psychologically or spiritually—easier to share our body than to share our fantasies, hopes, fears. . . . Hence people short-circuit the more "dangerous" building of a relationship by leaping immediately into bed. After all, the body is an object and can be treated mechanically.   —ROLLO MAY

It is no new thing to be lonely. It comes to all of us sooner or later. Friends die, families die. Lovers and husbands, too. We get old, we get sick. And the last and greatest loneliness is death. . . . It's a condition of man that we cannot escape. If we try to, we end in a darker hell. . . . But if we face it, if we remember that there are a million others like us, if we try to reach out to comfort them and not ourselves, we find in the end that we are lonely no longer. We are in a new family, the family of man.
—MORRIS WEST

The celibate priest or religious on the faculty of a Catholic college in these refreshingly frank days is an obvious target for a question like: "Don't you ever get lonely?" (My answer, of course, is, "Yes.") But doesn't everyone experience loneliness? It is certainly the state of many an unmarried person looking forward to marriage, and it's more poignantly the situation of the man or woman who must survive someone with whom they have shared life for decades. Sadly enough, it must be the case with the unhappily married. And isn't it also the situation of the happily married, to some degree? Does anyone seriously claim that even the happiest marriage eliminates all sense of the radical incommunicability of one's self?

This very incommunicability makes one hesitant about statements that include others, but there seems to be enough evidence in one cultural form or another to allow us to say that most of us feel this loneliness. Any human being who allows enough stillness to sound his or her own depths experiences at times that total ache that can best be described as the sense of being terribly, inescapably alone. Someone has pointed out well that every pain, every illness, every joy, every risk and decision in our lives, even the decision to join one's life to another and any other happy choice is surrounded by a circle that no other can enter and in which no one else can ever be the perfect counselor. And, we all die alone; no one does it for us or really does it with us.

Much great and less-great song and poetry is dominated by the theme of loneliness. Even the joyous hymns to love are joyous because they see love as the antidote to or the escape from loneliness and the absence of the loved one. Loneliness touches everyone from Shakespeare to Waylon Jennings. For Shakespeare: "All days are nights to see till I see thee." On a much more folksy level the pining lover sings: "I get tears in my eyes lying on my back thinking of you."

Loneliness is not accidental, not just a passing mood. We do, of course, use the term for flitting moments caused by such temporary causes as someone's absence. What is being discussed here, though, is something more persistent which is never dead, at the most only sleeping, ready to come to consciousness at any time; something for which there is no facile solution. The company of friends, the availability of pleasant companions, even the love of the one special person—none guarantee the easing of our loneness. And for some the fear of failing in those relations which lessen loneliness prevents even these consolations. T. E. Lawrence (of Arabia) wrote in his *Seven Pillars of Wisdom* about this, and the English poet A. E. Housman—probably speaking for many others—noted in the margin of his copy, "This is me."

There was my craving to be liked—so strong and nervous that never could I open myself to another. The terror of failure in an effort so important made me shrink from trying; besides, there was the standard; for intimacy seemed shameful unless the other could make the perfect reply, in the same language, after the same method, for the same reasons.

But loneliness, rooted in our strong sense of how incommunicable our deepest self is, is not merely a cause of pain; it is also a reason for pride. We are both blessed and burdened with an individual personality that we can never adequately disclose to or unite with another. The pain of separateness that hits us so hard is, no matter how searing, a consequence of our uniqueness, of the fact that we are not interchangeable, that none of us is completely transparent to another. Each of us is a mystery, not only to others but even to ourselves. The mystery stems from the incomparably inexhaustible richness of a human personality. We wonder how some fellow can sit gazing by the hour into the deep, dark pools of some young lady's eyes; he's simply trying to fathom that endless charm. Like everyone else she has depths that cannot be plumbed. Some are more acutely aware of this than others. The French novelist André Gide wrote: "Don't understand me too quickly." Our impenetrability is both our distinction and our cross. It is the spring of both our loneliness and our capacity for love.

(The whole matter of how much we do have in common and how we communicate it and share it is subject for another discussion. What is said here does not mean to deny that.)

Sadly enough, we are all familiar with some of the trashier escapes from loneliness: casual, cheap sex, carousing, drink and drugs, and more respectable ones like compulsive work or activity, avoidance of solitude and quiet. If genuine love and the assurance of an always-present spouse or family cannot stave off the ache, how much less these stand-ins?

From another point of view, if we are created in the image and likeness of God, it shouldn't be too surprising that it is no easy task for any human to know and love us as we'd like. In the euphoria of spring, youth, or a wedding, we can let pass the many outrageous claims made for human love. We sing: "Going to the chapel, and we're going to be married, and we'll never be lonely anymore." The loneliness which we learn does not go away that easily persists to teach us a number of important things about life. E.g., we have an apparently infinite capacity for love and understanding which goes way beyond anything we can ever receive from another human being. Our enduring sense of our solitariness should teach us to recognize some limits in what others can give us or be to us. In this latter insight lies, perhaps, part of the secret to greater longevity for marriage and friendship: this recognition that no one person can be everything to me that I could possibly desire or need.

We can learn from loneliness and we can learn to live with it. Banal and tritely maternal as it may sound to some, the advice to take an active interest in the good of others, to forget our own ache by turning our attention and energy to the needs of others, is sound advice. Concern for others certainly turns loneliness into a spur for good. To do this may take a kind of selflessness which the self-absorption of loneliness little inclines us to. But, on the other hand, pushing oneself into interest in those who seem to lack companionship or are neglected may be just the sort of action to turn us from excessive self-concern to something more altruistic. Here, too, as elsewhere in human life, it remains true that others do not exist simply to enhance or promote our spiritual growth; some sensitivity is needed. We cannot presume that everyone who appears lonely or in need of friends will regard you or me as what he or she has been waiting for all these years. They may not be that desperate! Still, in view of the demoralizing nature of loneliness for many, it is one of the consequences of God's love for us that we must risk something in showing some of that love for the desolate and neglected.

Further, loneliness highlights our need for friendship, our need for nonromantic friends alongside the relative exclusiveness of marriage and the family. Too much independence of others or a disdain for the effort and inconvenience that others introduce into a well-ordered life should not keep us from risking friendship. Like any other kind of love, the love of friends has its limitations but life without them is seriously truncated. Possibly an overemphasis on romantic love has diminished our appreciation for the comforts and unique solace to be found in people who qualify simply as friends.

Finally, our sense of the inadequacy of even the most intimate human relationship is meant, it seems to me, to drive us beyond the merely human. Our desires for intimacy and understanding are of such depth and insatiability that their adequate focus seems to be nothing less than God. And if God is to be the partner in a love or friendship, he must be conceived of as a person. Here we touch a central shock or scandal of Christianity: God did manifest himself to us and this through a specific human being whom we call Jesus Christ. No matter how many qualifications our reason may suggest about calling God a person or personal, it seems that the scriptural vision of him which we are given requires that he be at least personal, that the qualities of responsiveness and initiative be found in him in a surpassing degree. Someone has written: "To be a person is to be essentially in search of a person." Do not our fragmentary and unfulfilled loves point to the God who has revealed himself to us as person in Jesus Christ?

Implicit in all these essays is an acceptance of the belief that the human and the earthly are, in the Christian vision, good but not good enough. They serve to whet our appetite for a goodness which they reflect and also point to, God himself. The mystics who, over the centuries, have devoted so much of their time and effort to the cultivation of a personal and intimate relation to God in prayer may strike us as unbalanced. But, like any person who regards success, a high standard of living, the accumulation of things, etc., as all subsidiary to personal relationship, they have sought the one necessary thing which all our desires and disappointments serve to make real for us. In fact, one could argue that all our involvement in business, industry, academic life—work of any kind—is a way of filling up time that ideally would be spent in total and fulfilling personal intimacy.

At the very least, we should be driven to recognize that our relation to God must have some of the character of the personal and intimate, that even the best liturgical and/or public prayer is not enough to fulfill all the requirements of our relationship to God. To limit our relationship to the formal and social prayer of the community of believers can be (it need not be) similar to limiting our social intercourse with others to stock phrases to which we expect no genuinely individual responses. The acknowledgment that our hearts are seeking a deeper and more profound relationship than any human can assure us should lead to an eminently personal kind of prayer, a prayer so personal, in fact, that no one else can really suggest to us its style or manner.

To advocate that all of us should at least dip our toes into the cool and deep lake of mysticism is not to urge a return to simply God-and-me religion. Rather we stress that formal religion needs the balance of and the support of personal and uniquely individual religion expressed in my own irreplaceably private prayer to God perceived as the person capable of responding to me. Even the most socially oriented religion ultimately depends for its inspiration and sustenance on the motivation of a deeply personal relationship. Irretrievably romantic as it sounds (and why shouldn't the romantic express the central truths of human life as well as or better than what is called the "realistic"?), the driving force behind every great and good human action seems to be love, loyalty, devotion to a person or Person. The fact that the aches and pain of loneliness can lead us to closer intimacy with the "absolute" Person fits well with the other fact that we do our best and are sustained most enduringly in any good work by the assurance that an "absolute" Lover loves us.

Cloudy Days and Discouraging Words

It is not what you are or have been that God looks at with his merciful eyes, but what you would be. —*The Cloud of Unknowing*

Who reaches his ideal thereby surpasses it. —FRIEDRICH NIETZSCHE

If I could write the beauty of your eyes
And in fresh numbers number all your graces,
The age to come would say, "This poet lies!
Such heavenly touches ne'er touch'd earthly faces." —SHAKESPEARE

If youth be a defect, it is one that we outgrow only too soon.
—JAMES RUSSELL LOWELL

Love brings out the high and hidden qualities of the lover, his rare, exceptional states. Hence it easily deceives us about his ordinary ways.
—FRIEDRICH NIETZSCHE

Much of the idealism of the American myth is summed up in the stories and songs of the Old West. "Oh, give me a home where the buffalo roam and the deer and the antelope play." With equally American realism it has been said: "Give me a home where the buffalo roam and I'll show you a sloppy housekeeper." But no matter what reservations we have about that history (and North American Indians certainly have some), the song looks back to an idealized time when human nature and even the weather seem to have been different. "Where seldom was heard a discouraging word and the skies were not cloudy all day." From the movies we know too that the heroes were all honest and handsome, rugged and reserved, the heroines all blushing and beautiful, and the desperadoes always got the bad noose in the end.

Idealizing a previous period seems a constant tendency of humans. Within a few years of the resurrection the early Christians were gilding

104

their own first days. We read this description of their life in the Acts of the Apostles (2:42-47a):

> And they devoted themselves to the apostles' teaching and fellowship, to the breaking of bread and the prayers.
> And fear came upon every soul; and many wonders and signs were done through the apostles. And all who believed were together and had all things in common: and they sold their possessions and goods and distributed them to all, as any had need. And day by day, attending the temple together and breaking bread in their homes, they partook of food with glad and generous hearts, praising God and having favor with all the people.

They lived, in this description, in rosy-hued harmony and constant prayer, in an extraordinary unity which went to the extent of sharing all they had. They lived in the afterglow of the Lord's resurrection, filled with joy and praise, loved and honored by all.

In our society the family, family life, and married life are often presented—at least by TV family shows, schmalzy art, religious writers, celibate preachers, and entertainers turned evangelists—in similarly soft and glowing colors. And this despite all the truly terrifying figures about family and marital breakdown, despite the long history of intrafamily quarreling and tragedy. There is enough hypocrisy and lack of realism in pious and popular talk about the family to warrant giving the other side its due.

Let us look at a few "discouraging words" for a moment. Russian writer Leo Tolstoy's experience of "war and peace," for instance, was not limited to the military battlefield or the pages of his novel, at least not the war part. He wrote from experience when he said elsewhere that every unhappy family is unhappy in its own way. His own family life was a unique form of constant combat. Any reader of an account of his life will be ready to excuse Tolstoy and his wife from hell and even a stop in purgatory. They had simulated the pain associated with those terms well enough in their own home. The stereotypical scenes of family strife in a Fellini film, by comparison, are quite lighthearted though they, too, suggest a reality far from peace and harmony. The overidealized picture of family life that has become a standard prop of our commercial Christmases is utterly unrealistic by comparison. The twelve days of Christmas are—for some families—spent more often in carping than in caroling.

C. S. Lewis, too, has illustrated all of this. He relates the story of a minister friend whom he had heard preach very loftily about the family. The unreality of it all struck him because he had been at the minister's home shortly before. At the door the daughter had met him with: "For

God's sake, if they ask you to lunch, stay; it's always a little less frightful when there's a visitor." Family life, like any other segment of human life, calls for healing and redemption.

To get back to the early Christians. We know from the later chapters of the Acts of the Apostles that the fervor and unalloyed peace of that picture of the first believers was destined to be tarnished. Elsewhere in the same book we read of bickering, smallness, self-seeking, divisions, and persecutions. The ideal remained but it had to embrace the fact of failure and human imperfection.

What does all this mean for us or say to us? Are we to abandon ideals or be cynical about the vision of Christian community presented in Acts or about the ideal of Christian family living? Do we treat family and community life with the same skepticism we often bring to the political scene?

While we may not be able to live the ideal depicted in Acts and realize how far short of the ideal our own family life is, we do need idealism; we need ideals, hope, and vision. We need (1) to have some experience of the ideal possibilities, some vision of what could be, should be, might be, and (2) we need, not cynicism, but realism, some ability to forgive and understand, not to demand the impossible of others. We need an idealism that persists through the onslaughts of disappointment and heartbreak.

Our vision, our fortifying and sustaining experience must be, as for the early Christians, a vision of the power and presence of the risen Lord in our lives. We will not have the joyous life we desire and that modicum of peace which we require apart from a strong confidence in the presence, here and now in our lives, of the risen Lord. In him and the power of the resurrection the transformation of our world has begun. That he is risen and lives always is our assurance against the ultimate triumph of death and evil and our help in darkness and doubt, our guarantee that cynicism and despair are not justified. It is the ultimate basis for the essential realism of Christian optimism and idealism.

Recent decades have shown us the fragility of idealism and hope built on the shifting sands of confidence in human nature and better societal organization. How many of the disappointed cynics and contented bourgeoisie of today are the raving idealists of the sixties grown older? Only a hope and confidence built on the continual power and presence of the risen Lord in our creation can sustain us in our search for better lives, better worlds, better communities.

We need at some moment to have glimpsed or felt the reality of the ideal we have in our hearts of either Christian life or, more specifically, of family, married, community life. We need ideals, a vision, even an idealistic vision, of what life, marriage, community can be. The fervor and even wild expectations of youth should not too easily be dismissed or transcended—if indeed they can be. In the resurrection we have reasons for idealism and hope, not just beyond death but here and now. But for this to be real means we must have experienced to some degree the abiding joy that can come from living in the risen Christ.

In the process we need to distinguish the Christian ideal of life, marriage, and family from the impossible dream, the dishonest romanticizing, or the unreal expectations of life and of other people. In the Samaritan woman of chapter 4 of St. John's Gospel and in her many counterparts in our civilization we see illustrated a hunger which is exorbitant, built on unrealistic expectations. It is instructive for us. Christ answers the woman's thirst, demonstrated by a succession of husbands or paramours, by telling her that if she knew who he was and what he could do she would drink from the water he would give that becomes in those who believe a fountain springing up to eternal life. May not the Christian's solution be found in shifting the attention from *our* desires—our expectation of *others* in regard to love and family—to our expectation of what *Christ can be for us* and what, through his grace, *we ourselves* can bring to the problems of life? We may, perhaps, need to ask much more of Christ, much more of ourselves and, correspondingly, not demand the impossible of others.

If Christ is in any sense to become in our life what he should be we must set the stage, prepare the way. Here that idealistic picture in Acts may be able to suggest some things we can "do." If those verses do not tell what *was*, i.e., history—that is seldom Scripture's main interest— they do propose what *should* be. (1) We must "devote" ourselves "to the apostles' teaching"; the intellectual element of our faith must be nourished. We owe some study to the faith that comes to us from the apostles. Reading and study, reflection and seeking are not optional, especially for those who are capable of them in other areas of their lives. (2) The apostolic Christians did not, it seems clear, sense an absolute obligation to total communion of property and goods but they did recognize an obligation to the less fortunate, the poor. In other words, the intellectual apprehension of the faith must be accompanied by doing the word, by the exercise of the love and concern for the poor and the lowly which has always marked the ideal Christian.

(3) ". . . breaking bread in their homes, they partook of food with glad and generous hearts." "Breaking bread" is a New Testament term for sharing the Lord's Supper. Our faith and its endurance must be rooted

in a sharing of the Eucharist and a realization of its character as a communal meal signifying oneness with Christ and with each other, a celebration of fellowship. We have far to go in reforming an immoderately private Jesus-and-me vision of the Eucharist. (4) "And day by day, attending the temple together . . . praising God." Prayer must be accepted as the irreplaceable environment of a truly Christian life. Without it we make impossible the action of God through which he is able to transform us and enliven our sense of living in his risen Son.

Our willingness to practice such a program is what makes possible the experience that Jesus is risen and lives. This experience, it should be noted, cannot be too narrowly defined. What is being said here is not to be equated with "Go out and have a mystical experience." Depending on our temperamental makeup, the experience or conviction can vary immensely in intensity or concreteness. That Christ is risen and lives in and with us is never proved but it can be known by each of us in the same way that we know the love of another person. That experience is the honeymoon of the Christian life. Like the early happiness and joy of married people, like the early Christians' life in Christ, once sensed, it can remain vivid in our memory and heart to help us through the days when that sparkle and enthusiasm may be dimmed.

Easter and its permanence in us by means of prayer, Christian living, Eucharist, and intelligent apprehension of its content should bring us, as the years go by, a deeper and more solid joy and confidence. Only this can see us through the Novembers and Februaries, the disappointment, the drudgery, the rained-out games, the too-soon return of winter, the failures of friends, the letdown we sense at the hands of family, the failed tests, the disillusionment, the downright tragedies of human life. Though we have not seen him, we can know, by dint of a faith truly lived and generously practiced, the joy, the peace, and the life that comes to those who dare to believe and trust. That experience can reaffirm for us that the often brash idealism and unmitigated hope of the young is closer to the mark than any tired hopelessness or cynicism.

Person to Person

No human being can be really himself in a world of things; to reach his proper selfhood he has to meet another whom he addresses as Thou. In crying out, "Thou," he is for the first time himself an "I."   —MARTIN D'ARCY

By following Jesus Christ man in the world today can truly humanly live, act, suffer and die; in happiness and unhappiness, life and death, sustained by God and helpful to man.   —HANS KÜNG

If we are going to have a god at all, let us have "Our Father which art in heaven." Look at Matthew Arnold with his "stream of tendency, by which all things seek to fulfill the law of their being." In some way or other the abstract exists, no doubt, but the point is that the mind does not desire the abstract, it desires the thing.... If we want God, we want him as a Father, not as a stream of tendency, and this is the secret of the power of Christianity. Its so-called anthropomorphism is nothing less than the nature of the mind which cannot be satisfied with anything but whole things.
—R. H. BLYTH

The believer, like the lover, has no conclusive proofs to give him complete security. But the believer too, like the lover, can be completely certain of the Other by committing himself entirely to the Other. And this certainty is stronger than all the security established by proofs.   —HANS KÜNG

In a book called *The Decline and Fall of Sex*, Robert Fitch wrote that marriage was only necessary in the contemporary novel as a precondition for the ever-present adultery. Scripture itself indicates that the two, marriage and unfaithfulness, have coexisted for thousands of years with adultery possibly only a few months younger. Scripture scholar John McKenzie thinks that marriages arranged by a business agreement, as was common in societies such as that of the ancient Jews, must inevitably have resulted in many loveless marriages and hence much incentive to infidelity.

109

But marital faithfulness and its violation, adultery, have a more comprehensive significance throughout Scripture than that envisioned in the commandment against adultery. The Hebrew Scriptures—for example, Ezekiel and Hosea—are replete with the language of marriage and unfaithfulness. God's people are regarded as his bride; their marriage contract, their agreement, is the covenant. Turning to other gods—what would be called, strictly speaking, apostasy or idolatry—is castigated by the prophets as unfaithfulness or adultery.

All this presupposes that we are modeling God, the other party, after human persons as we know them and in relations of love. That presupposition deserves to be more than taken for granted, although, in another sense, it is certainly a testimony to a kind of common and divine sense that we *do* assume that God is person and our relations with him personal. We might do more with the conception were we to see deeper into its richness. Despite our assumption that God is person or is personal, as we understand the term, we too easily settle for a model of religious behavior which is anything but personal. Or if it is personal, it is on the model of personal as seen in the encounter, for instance, of lawgiver and subject, judge and defendant. This may have some validity but it has greater limitations. And such a relationship, of course, is not behind the talk about the possibility of faithfulness or unfaithfulness. We may be disobedient to the lawgiver or resistant to the judge but we would hardly call that adultery. The latter presupposes a personal relationship of mutuality, love, respect, commitment, even intimacy.

Often the dull and wearying thing about being a Catholic Christian has been the idea so often accepted without question that it means belonging to another huge organization with laws and regulations. Most of us of necessity belong to enough such societies as it is—our country, municipality, county, the company or army, an athletic or recreational club, the condominium or apartment complex. And all have rules for us, the members: Parking is permitted on the right side of Schmelzer Avenue only between 9 A.M. and 5 P.M.—No Pets allowed.—Garbage must be separated and bagged by item.—Income tax returns are due April 15.—Packages of such items cannot contain in addition a personal letter.—If your name begins with the letters *A* to *K*, please board the plane now.

We don't need a religion patterned on the legal ideal; but church leaders did, in fact, succumb to the desire to so model the church, especially in the late middle ages. The results: not just church laws (canon law) but a tendency to multiply regulations in many areas of Christian life.

If we think about all this in the light of the Gospels we realize that the most ardent followers of the Lord we meet there are people attracted by the person of Jesus, that embodiment of God's love for us and of our perfect response to that love. Once attracted to him their ideal became to live as loyalty would demand. There's a certain naturalness about that, a conformity without deeper experience. A. E. Housman speaks for our experience of the power of personal attraction:

> Oh, when I was in love with you,
>   Then I was clean and brave,
> And miles around the wonder grew
>   How well did I behave.

The Shropshire Lad, XVIII

But then we hear ourselves saying: "Sure, that's ideal but romantic, even unrealistic. We don't see the Lord." "I'll do well if I just learn the rules and try to follow them." "A personal relationship to Jesus may be all right for a mystic or someone in a cloister with plenty of time . . . or for someone with that kind of temperament."

Or we claim to like the laws and regulations because they make it all so much more manageable and neat. You know when you've done your part (tithing, for instance); you can look at the rules periodically and clear your conscience. "I haven't killed anyone today. I've been to Mass every Sunday."

The church tried to move away from much of that with the Second Vatican Council. Under the impact of biblical studies and the good example of many other Christians, this legalism of the church was seen as inadequate at the very least. Getting away from all that was certainly a breath of that fresh air John XXIII wanted to let into the church when he conceived the idea of the Council.

But some, rather than sensing the liberation in all this, have felt lost. Who's to tell me or help me spell out what to do? How much to do? When to do it? Such complaints owe their existence to the bad education the church's legalism gave so many of us. The overall impact of the Gospels and the New Testament does not lead us to expect that a neat set of regulations would replace the legalism Jesus opposed in the religion of his time.

Nostalgia for minute regulations is hard to square with Christianity's ideals. Thanks to a general ignorance of the New Testament many a Catholic would never realize that. While Matthew's Gospel may present Jesus as the new Moses, the new lawgiver, the "laws" he gives are rather ideals and goals than rules and are placed in distinct contrast with the existent legalism and literalism. (See the Sermon on the Mount, Matt 5-7.) Christian tradition at its best, echoed for example in the prefaces of the

Christmas liturgy, has understood the incarnation and life of Jesus as a way for God to attract our love. Through the visibility of that earthly life we are to be drawn to the love of the invisible God that Jesus pictures.

Living solely in terms of regulations and laws is but another way we dehumanize our lives: in this case, specifically, our relationship to God. It is an attempt to quantify what must be unquantifiable, individually unique. The efforts to define human existence as the relationship of things, of quantities, of numbers, are always present. The materialist and those who overextend the methodology of science do it in their way. They define the human being in the limited ways that formulas, measurements, and appearance allow. Legalism in the church does it in another way. In all these efforts we miss and attempt to avoid the joys, risks, doubts, satisfaction, and messiness that follow from relationships of love, admiration, trust. And we eventually lose or destroy our humanness. It should be obvious how we reduce ourselves when we seek to find satisfaction or fulfillment in things (objects) or define ourselves in terms of them. Our dignity and destiny as persons—free, responsible, unpredictable, beings capable of thought and love—are maintained and even realized only in concert with other humans, in personal relationships.

So true is this that the Christian tradition has always seen God as at least personal, as having the best qualities we attribute to persons. We say "at least personal," since we cannot know his mode of existence. We mean that he can elicit the loyalty and love of human beings. In religion as in human life in general, we respond to the assurance that we are loved. Once loved, we more easily love. Possibly this needs to be stressed, first of all, on the level of our ordinary human relationships.

The situation of the "busy" person who cuts off human contacts or reduces them significantly because there is "no time" is not just sad; it is tragic. And so often humanity is the chief casualty in our pursuit of comfort, position, prestige. But can we really expect to be fully human if we leave out or seriously curtail the specifically human elements in our existence? Similar to the impoverished life of the person who is content to live among things and objects is that of the Christian who will not graduate from a life determined by rules and laws to one of personal following of Jesus Christ.

God has gone out of his way, we might say, to ask such a personal, loving response from us. One facet of the inexhaustible mystery we celebrate at Christmas is that God has given his love, faithfulness, and concern for us a face, figure, eyes, ears, and hands. He became one of us. We are much too used to that expression and similar ones to fully realize the unheard-of character of it all. It deserves our pondering.

Granted that the incredibility of the incarnation stems partly from its seeming to us to be too good to be true, it does, by the same token, have a comprehensibility about it. It corresponds to what we are and how we act. (Parenthetically, it might be pointed out that there seems no more improbability in God acting *in accordance* with our nature and aspirations than in his acting at cross purposes to our desires. A God who loves us and condescends to us is not intrinsically more improbable than one who would be an ogre or indifferent.) No matter how much we allow ourselves to live in numbers, abstractions, and laws, we all ache for the less neat reality and actual embraceability of a person, a three-dimensional being able to attract us and, in turn, respond to us. We do our best for Cathy or Bill: we endure, often, even the figures, abstractions, mechanisms, computers, and paperwork of daily life because we know there is someone with whom we can share some distinctly human moments of companionship, love, conversation.

In view of all this, did God really have any choice but to incarnate himself in Jesus Christ?

Love or Legalism

In terms of our response we apparently do think that *we* have a choice. E.g., we can follow a collection of laws and regulations and make that the sum and substance of our relation to God. *Or* we can learn to grow in love for him through the vision and presence of Jesus Christ given to us in Scripture, prayer, the liturgy, and life with our fellow human beings. But is that really the choice? Is a religion of legalism sufficient in any sense of the word, at least for self-conscious, maturing, somewhat informed persons in this century? Is not the choice more likely to be between a religion founded in love and discipleship and a non-existent, unsatisfying, or wilting religion based on law? Even though the personal following of Jesus, apprehended in our own conscience and not simply or only mediated to us by church or laws or regulations, has more risks, is ultimately more demanding, and appeals more to our responsibility, it is still more likely to arouse in us lifelong fidelity than the alternative.

And the object of our following, of our love, is, on his side, unable to be unfaithful. That his love is eternal, endless, and unchanging, not subject to destruction by our failures; that unfaithfulness can never be on his side: all this is not just a message of both the Hebrew Scriptures and the New Testament but is *the* perduring message. On our side, of course, there is—as in all personal relationships—the possibility of unfaithfulness, a failure of love and generosity.

The possibilities of such relationships are put before us whenever we witness a wedding, the celebration of the promises made by two people to each other. On such an occasion we see the beauty, daring, and generosity of people committing themselves to each other, promising faithfulness, making a "covenant." We need constant reflection on this both for the sake of our life with others and for the sake of putting some of the same spirit into our relationship with God. What Gabriel Marcel wrote of this has application to our context:

> In swearing fidelity to a person, I do not know what future awaits us or even, in a sense, what person he or she will be tomorrow. The very fact of not knowing is what gives worth and weight to my promise.

In a world of meanly calculated deals, of wheeler-dealers cognizant of every little bit that is their due, taking into account every possible risk, the spectacle of two people pledging themselves to an unknown future is refreshing, an assurance that generosity and self-forgetting persist. Somewhere Friedrich Nietzsche defines human beings as the only beings capable of making promises, something we do not expect from chihuahuas and chimpanzees or even of children below a certain age, something that deserves celebration.

Where the risk and daring are in a relationship to God is not as obvious as a first glance might suggest. We risk no danger of unreturned love—his love for us began before we were born—but God certainly risks failures on our part. He has risked himself over and over again: in creating free persons in the first place and not least in the incarnation. He risks himself with each one of us. We risk ourselves insofar as the implications of our commitment become evident only with the passage of time, the maturing of our faith. As the open-endedness of the Sermon on the Mount indicates, our love and relation to God are capable of making ever greater demands on us. Eventually we see things to be done or not done which would have been incomprehensible to us when we "first met."

Our baptism signalized for most of us the beginning of our relationship. Promises were made by us or for us to the Father. Only time tells us the implications. As in the case of marriage, so in the case of something so momentous as religious commitment, a pledge of faithfulness cannot be totally blind. The two parties in the marriage have discussed tastes and aspirations; they do know how the other feels about mushrooms, Mozart, mutual funds, and manners. They have some idea of what to expect.

Yet, even given some adequate knowledge, the promise of faithfulness is deeper, more far-reaching than its reasons. The implications of faithfulness go beyond what can simply be justified by calculation. The question will always be there for the observer or outsider: What do they see in each other? To expect scientific certitude about the other party before pledging fidelity could easily lead to one of those fabled and inevitably somewhat tragic thirty-year courtships. Fidelity means suspending doubts out of trust in the mutually constructive power of promises to overcome hesitancy. Faithfulness engenders faithfulness, trust builds trust, love strengthens love. We would certainly err to omit knowledge completely, and we would err to expect too much of it. Once again, one needs to defer to experience: those in love are best able to understand the mixture of knowledge and uncertainty and commitment that goes into a relationship.

In many of these essays the reader will notice an emphasis—rather constant, it is hoped—on the necessity for each one of us to assume responsibility for his or her own reply to the grace of God, for informing him or herself sufficiently, for nourishing the life of the Spirit. I have hoped to avoid any suggestion that others, including this writer, can do this *for us*. A certain amount of knowledge is our responsibility. Drawing the proper conclusions from knowledge for action is also our responsibility. As our human relationships require effort, sacrifice, and even ingenuity to grow, so our relationship to Christ and to the Father, already a matter of repeated initiative on God's part, requires that we show some corresponding openness and concern to learn, to deepen our faith and our love.

The means to this relationship are so obvious as to be almost painful to detail: reading, studying, meditating the Scriptures (especially the Gospels), genuine prayer, participation in the sacraments and worship and life of the community of Christians, and loving concern and action on behalf of others in the world. Knowing the world we live in, its problems of oppression, starvation, unjust and immoral competition, and acting as our circumstances and talents allow—all these must follow our commitment. Once we see that our faith is not exhausted by a set of rules and observances, the following of Jesus becomes better focused, the implications clearer.

Possibly it is necessary to stress that the *love* of Christ is not something different from what we have been discussing. Love means the identification with what the loved one sees as good, an orientation of one's life in accordance with the good of the loved one. Since we tend so easily to equate love with its emotional accompaniments, present at times, there may be some reluctance to use the term for our relationship with the Lord. We feel it's a bit too dramatic, a bit overdone. But even in our ordinary use of the term, we understand or must learn that love can be present even when the emotional delight seems absent. All the more in the love of the unseen God, the element of excitement and feeling may be absent much of the time. It is almost platitudinous to remark that human experience can be adduced to show that love is more often proved by what it does and endures than by what it protests and sings—delightful as the latter may be. In any case, love with or without its emotional fireworks never asks how much to do for the beloved; it doesn't consult a guide book in order to know what to do next.

In the life, cross, death, and resurrection of Jesus, the Father has underlined graphically the truth of his unfailing love for us. All of Christian life amounts to an effort to respond adequately and in our own unique way to that love given us by another person. Nothing else in institutions or laws can approach the absolute claim of that love on us.

Ideally our response should be equally absolute, and in the life of Christ in us, grace, there is the increasing possibility of more and more adequate response, response without hesitation. For most of us the response will have to be gradual, at times disappointing and meager, but unless it is at least in process something is seriously lacking to our would-be discipleship.

Once More with Repentance

Spiritual Flashing. The box was the one place where I could fling open my overcoat and reveal my soul. It wasn't my idea—the Church absolutely insisted on it. "Take it off, take it all off." Until, like a shy girl doing a striptease in an icehouse, I stood shaking before the impressario himself. And the Big Fellow would nod his blue jowls and grunt, "OK, kid—I've seen worse. Next, please."   —WILFRID SHEED

Sin is not one mere action, but it is an attitude to life which takes it for granted that our goal is finite, that our self is the ultimate truth, and that we are not all essentially one but exist each for his own separate individual existence.   —RABINDRANATH TAGORE

He (the Christian) is always moving beyond his refusals and pressing forward to what lies ahead. In the incomprehensibiltiy of his own dark and obscure freedom he knows that he is always encompassed by God's grace, and he knows that he must always take refuge in this grace of God. He is always a person who does not add up his account before God, but rather he leaves to God and to his grace all of his accounts, and all of the moral struggles and moral trials which were imposed upon him and which of course he cannot ultimately "judge."   —KARL RAHNER

Being reminded every two seconds that one is OK may be necessary as an effective counter to pietistic guilt (or a real help for those with psychic problems) but for most Christians it's far sounder to operate in the context of forgiveness—to know that God accepts people with shortcomings. We might better say, "I'm not OK, you're not OK, but that's OK."
—*The Lutheran*

Honesty or falsehood, chastity or unchastity, love or egoism are ultimately realized in a whole life or a period of it, and seldom display themselves clearly in any particular act. Hence the confession of one's sins must rather

117

be a life discerned than acts listed. . . . And the deepest sin is a resistance to the summons to rise up from our daily falls humbly and hopefully.
—PIET SCHOONENBERG

"Let's Quit Pretending about Birth Control" was the title of an article in a Catholic magazine a few years ago, and it suggested a title for an article about the sacrament of penance, commonly called confession. "Let's Quit Pretending about Confession." If that isn't clear, then what do I mean? Let's not try to fool ourselves—people are not going to confession these days. If you haven't noticed, just check it out with those a bit younger than yourself. The good old Saturday afternoon confession lines have gone the way of men's garters, nickel candy bars and black-and-white television. The lines are now at the supermarket. Admittedly penitents may persist in some isolated pockets of Catholic America. There, in my experience, the pastor often prides himself on insisting on the old rules and practices, and the visiting priest hears confessions about "missing grace before meals fourteen times since my last confession two weeks ago." And the pastor clucks over the number of confessions, more testimony that the quantitative and often magical approach to religion is fiercely persistent, from the days of counting indulgences till now.

Anywhere, even in the confessional or reconciliation room itself, the refrain is: "I don't believe in confession." People mean specifically the practice of confessing sins individually to a priest for absolution, forgiveness. The falling off in the practice of confession is due to some lack of belief rather than to the fact that we've all become such models of sinless perfection.

To be more specific, my experience suggests that the lack of belief touches two matters. (1) The notion that one would rarely get through the week without at least a mortal sin or two and, as a corollary, that one is ordinarily in more danger of hell than of being hit by a religious beggar in an airport. (2) The idea that the priest is somehow essential for one's forgiveness.

The conception of mortal or serious sin dominant in Catholic practice in recent centuries gave the impression that these sins were such objective "things" that we could just go to the list in the back of a prayerbook to find which ones we happened to have hit, and forthwith we knew how many mortal sins we had committed. To claim that such a picture is exaggerated is to retrospectively whitewash a reality many of us knew well. This notion trivialized serious sin, suggested that one fell in and out of a state of grace or friendship with God with the same ease with which one changed socks. It certainly helped lessen the gap—were that so desirable!—between some heinous torturer of thousands of people and the ordinary Christian who had paged through *Playboy* or missed Sunday Mass. This conception, despite some good Catholic tradition and teaching to the contrary, ignored the mitigating effects of habit, ignorance, lack of reflection, and the value or importance of the overall orientation of one's life. Psychology as we know it today did not discover these factors but it probably has helped revitalize otherwise forgotten bits of wisdom in the Christian tradition.

The other problem for belief is that one's sins are not really forgiven (forget all the befogging explanations about how one is forgiven by God just by being sorry but nevertheless is obliged to go to confession also) unless one has followed the formula and brought them orally to the attention of Father McGillicuddy. For years the best theology has attempted to explain this necessity in terms of Father representing not only God who forgives but the community which has been offended or sinned against by us and with which we need reconciliation. Militating against these ideas is some confusion about how necessary Father is if God is willing to forgive always and anywhere and, allied to this, a difficulty in seeing Father as so simply, solely, and surely representing our community.

Undoubtedly there is much to be rediscovered and appropriated in these two allied notions but, like all truths or insights, they need their time and milieu and I do not think it is here and now. They are just very difficult to see for modern Christians. Good theologians and preachers cannot just state well these beliefs and hope that forthwith we are going to have compliance. More is required. Possibly—without going into a broad historical and worldwide survey—it can be said that the church, from the side of her ministers at least, has to somehow reestablish a credibility that will make it more easily seen as representative of God and the community. Finally, the lack of belief may be related to the difficulty contemporary Christians have in accepting as even Christian such minute specifications of God's will for us, the imposition of such legalism on Christian life, i.e., sins must be confessed by number and species, etc.

I suspect that the official church will catch up with the practice and belief of vast numbers of Catholics (as it has so often in other matters), and we will arrive at a situation in which the church's minister will declare to a group, with or without individual confession, that they are forgiven—what is called general absolution. This is already provided for in the legislation that still surrounds the sacrament, though with such cumbersome restrictions that it takes a hardy bishop to countenance it without fear of Roman rumblings. Historically there have been various ways in which the church has announced to believers their forgiveness by God in Christ. Confession in the form known in recent centuries in the Western Roman Catholic church has not been present everywhere and at all times. (There is no reason to give any credence to the stories about Joseph making confessionals in his carpenter's shop.) The early church seems to have used ecclesiastical absolution only in cases of apostasy, murder, or adultery.

There is an ecumenical consensus on what is probably essential in the whole matter: Protestant and Catholic theology seem pretty well agreed that one of the essential tasks of the church is to proclaim to believers that God does forgive our sins, that love from his side is not destroyed by unfaithfulness on our part, and that this must be announced in and out of season. The "how" of the proclamation is at issue and up for discussion if not for substantial revision in the Roman church.

"More like a carwash than an overhaul" is the way someone has described the traditional (i.e., practice of our most recent centuries) confession. We came to confession with our lists, like shopping lists, of sins such as: I got drunk three times; I missed Mass twice; I spoke harshly to my husband four times a week, etc. We rattled them off, heard a few words from the priest, expressed our sorrow, were given a penance of five Hail Marys, received absolution, and left. What was confessed was a series of omissions and commissions. Rarely did they concern the causes or circumstances in which we took advantage of the generosity of others or from which our anger, excessive drinking, or cheating took place or rarely did they touch the core aspirations of our spiritual life.

Confession of our particular, personal, and most private sins to a priest most likely developed from the practice of medieval (possibly Irish) monks of confessing their most personal failing to a spiritual advisor or father in order to get help toward making some spiritual progress. Somewhere along the line this became the official, mandated, and very systematized practice of the church. Without trying to solve the matter of our present widespread disbelief in confession and nonpractice of it, I believe we can agree that each of us needs to assess his or her life and actions and this with some regularity and frequency. We may even be ready to admit that help with this can come from speaking to another person. That seems basic—to know ourselves—whether it results in a sacramental confession or not. One of many students who have confessed their nonconfessing to me added these significant words: "That doesn't mean I don't evaluate myself at times." That we can and must do, and with this my remaining words will be concerned.

More than drawing up lists of sins with mathematical accuracy, our growth in Christ requires seeing the underlying attitudes and traits that lead us to specific offenses. For example, it would be more important to note that we haven't really prayed sincerely in months than that we have omitted morning prayers seven times; that we have taken for granted others' time and the use of their property; that we have failed to respect others' dignity and integrity when our own sexual desires were involved; that we've wasted whole weeks in aimless playing around, but haven't had time to just talk with or recreate with people who like us and appreciate our company; that we've ignored the depression or sorrow of friends and neighbors which might have disturbed our tranquility had we inquired.

What would make such an examination most helpful would be the effort to get at the general direction of our lives, some analysis of our motives, of our priorities, of our intentions. We could ask ourselves, for instance: Does Christ really have *the* important role or any important role in my life? Have I grown since leaving school or marrying? Do I have any ideal of what kind of person I'd like to be or should be? How do I act toward those I'm closest to? What impact does some resolution made years ago or some great experience still have on my life? Do I take any responsibility for our society, for the world around me, for my neighborhood or environment, for the tone of life and recreation with my friends? Have I been ready to commit myself to action at some expense to my ease and preferences? Is my religion or religious practice perfunctory, mechanical, magical? Is my usual attitude toward life hopeful, trusting, cynical, constructive, hopeless, destructive? Does the fast pace of the years urge me to "grab more gusto" or give more to life, to those around me, to the present? Answering or facing similar questions would, it seems to me—and my experience with face-to-face confessions of college students confirms this—give some depth to our Christian life. And, should it lead to that, it would greatly improve any sacramental confession we might make. Reviewing our life two or three times a year with the help of some such examination could make for some constructive growth, could indicate some effort to take my life in Christ more seriously.

The ancient custom of preparing for Christmas and Easter with some sort of renewal of the Christian life deserves to survive, itself renewed. Before both great celebrations we have seasons that urge us to repudiate our sins and ask forgiveness. To recognize sin, failure, guilt—I have done what I know I should not have done— this is really just the other side of responsibility, freedom. "If we say we have no sin we deceive ourselves, the truth is not in us. . . . If we say we have not sinned, we make him a liar, and his word is not in us" (1 John 1:8-10).

The redemption and salvation we celebrate at Christmas and Easter make little sense apart from an evaluation of our lives which makes us face responsibility. The self-knowledge involved in such a recognition may be one of the elementary phases in a Christian life. But just for that reason we should be certain that we are not omitting it, that it is there. Otherwise we are easily self-deceived and strangers to the truth about ourselves and, consequently, about the one who saves us from ourselves, from sin and death.

Table Talk

High religion always includes, of course, a summons to above-average morality, but it is a fatal blunder to assume that its eyes are fixed primarily on this summons. Its attention is on a vision which, almost incidentally and as a by-product, sets morality in motion.   —HUSTON SMITH

It may be the Baptist in me—still in me, thank God—which causes Catholics' talk about liturgy to turn me off, as if the purpose of worship were less prayer than production. But we who try to live as Christians need a holy fix about once a week. We need to hear the word preached to stir us up. We need music that turns the mind and heart to prayer. We need a sense that we are at worship among brothers and sisters. We need the Lord's Supper.   —THOMAS L. SCHAFFER

The most powerful motive is love of a person. The New Testament tells of that Person "whom you love without seeing." This is the fundamental meaning of the "faith" which Christ requires, this self-giving to his Person and message which describes the normal Christian attitude.
—R. RUSSELL

To a frustrating degree and frequently one hears people talking as if being a Christian primarily had to do with not killing, not fleecing friends or foes, not stealing wives or real estate. Most religions agree, somewhere in their teaching, that these matters are wrong and this essay will not dispute that. The last five or six commandments (depending on the numbering) of the Jewish and Christian Ten—touching these matters— can be duplicated in many other religions with but slight variations. Such morality, evidently, is not distinctively Christian or Jewish. What is unique to these religions of Semitic origin, what should be prior in our esteem, is something else. It is embodied in the first three or four commandments which refer to God: he is the one and only God; he is to be reverenced; his worship is given priority in a day set aside for him and it. Recognizing in thought and act God's foremost place in our lives is basic to everything else. We rightly assume that all this is somehow tied to whether or not one cheats, steals, or kills.

How the praise of God and its priority are related to conduct is no simple matter. At times the commands about moral behavior are seen as conditions for worship, the necessary conduct that fits us for it. For instance, Jesus says that before going to the altar to offer our gift we should be reconciled with our neighbor. And Christian worship begins ordinarily with a confession of sin and prayer for forgiveness. But that isn't the whole story. Good morals also are seen as the self-evident consequence of good worship, the ethics that follow from a right and prior relation to God. Apparently it works both ways: a good life, a sensitive conscience, makes us better prepared for the encounter with God. *And* our meeting with God in turn should fuel our desire to live as he wills, to love as he does, to "imitate" him. In either case the hub of the wheel of Christian life is worship and God's primary place in our existence.

Humanly speaking, the worship of God is a strange activity, one that is a puzzle to common sense and rationality. What is stranger than a group of people gathered together to address someone they can't see? It is the one activity in which the churches have no competition—strictly speaking. Their unique concern is worship, the worship of God. We need to add that "of God" otherwise we *do* run into genuine forms of competition warned against in the first commandment. There *are* such things as self-worship and the worship of wealth, force, race, success, nation, peace of mind, security.

"Tell me to what you pay attention and I will tell you who you are," someone has written. One should be able to recognize a Christian by the primary place God has in his or her life and the effects apparent in comportment. The distinctively Hebraic commandments aim to assure that God is first in our hearts and lives. Idolatry is not obsolete: while we may not worship gold idols, the gold itself is another matter. Idolatry persists as a, *the,* human failure in which we give some segment or element of our existence total and unquestioned loyalty and autonomy. We withdraw it from its true position as relative to God and our final destiny; we put it beyond question and appraisal from outside itself. We are idolaters when we accept the notion, for instance, that our economic dealings are not subject to moral evaluation, that making a profit is its own justification.

In Christianity the outward sign of our effort to assure primacy to God is our joining together in worship. *Effort* is the word because, of

course, we can through routine and lack of care make attendance at Mass
—like wearing a medal or mouthing "Jesus saves"—into a piece of magic
or a formality by which we excuse ourselves from visiting the sick or
paying our debts. Those who complain that regular churchgoers are
hypocrites can always point to examples in living color. Someone comes
out of church and sideswipes my car in the parking lot; the person who
sat in front of me pulls a shady financial deal the next day; I go home
and "raise hell" with the family over nothing. In practice, we all seem
devious enough to weasel out of the consequences of prayer and worship.
We can use regularity at Mass even—or maybe especially—when our
attendance is mechanical and half-hearted, as an excuse for neglecting
a discouraged or lonely friend, for thinking we *have* served God.

The fact that Christian worship so often, regularly for Catholics
and Orthodox, consists in the celebration of the Lord's Supper, the Eucharist, is germane to this matter of worship and conduct. The commemo-
ration of the Lord's death in the Eucharist points worship more defini-
tively to the link with generous behavior.

In another of these essays we make the point that sharing at the
table of the altar in the common meal should affect and solidify human
relations of love and friendship, even assure us of their possibility and
value. Here we should pay some attention to the fact that in celebrating
the Eucharist we are doing something Jesus told us to do in memory of
him. In giving that injunction he spoke of his body and blood handed
over for us or poured out for us. In more technical terms the church
recognized that the Eucharist is not only a memorial of the Last Supper,
that last gathering in love and companionship, but a memorial also of
the suffering and death that were to follow. We say the Mass is sacrificial,
a continuation, a representation, of the final and capping act of Jesus'
life of service and surrender to his Father and his destiny. We are to
share not only in the assurance of union with the Lord and each other
but also in the Lord's sacrificial will, his self-emptying life and spirit.
It is both consolation and crucifixion.

By linking worship of God with his life and activity—self-giving
and radical obedience to his destiny—Jesus attempts, insofar as our
devious natures make that possible, to tie praise and worship of God to
self-sacrifice and self-giving, to assure that we see worship as not simply
words and music but giving and doing, as a commitment to honor God
away from the altar by how we live and act. Taking part in the Mass
should help us in the never-ended task of learning to be Christians, to
become more like the teacher and Lord. The self-giving of Jesus on the
cross is the paradigm for our own and at the same time the source which

makes it possible. If we note that the words *disciple* and *discipline* are related in the Latin root to a word meaning to learn, then maybe *discipline* would be a good word for the whole process. For worship is meant —almost in passing—by dint of so much closeness to the Lord, to help form true disciples. Discipline involves learning from someone qualified how to do something: in this case, how to live and how to love. A teacher who is able to illustrate a lesson by dying on the cross is certainly, to understate it, a master of that craft or art.

At Mass we are all present as apprentices. The self-giving which is at the heart of being a disciple of Jesus and which we are gradually to learn there is not inborn in any sense of the word. If it is to be present, it must be acquired. To transform our natural tendency to self-indulgence into self-giving love and likeness to Christ takes time; it is rarely sudden. St. Benedict writes of life in the monastery as a "school of the Lord's service." One aspect of the Mass must be its function as the school of the Lord's service for believers.

Christ's teaching and Christian worship are based on a belief that we need help and exercise in loving others as we do ourselves. Worship and the practical love of others are related in such a way that worship without the love is empty. And, on the other hand, the effort to love, the ability to free ourselves from sheer self-seeking, is ultimately possible only by sharing Christ's offering. This is made present for us, not pictorially but powerfully, in every Eucharist. Worship is both the process and the place where the disciples of Christ have the word and the example of Jesus, in particular his death for others, continually put before their minds and hearts. It is here that our whole self can be nourished by the body and blood of Christ, the Word made flesh.

The Gospel about being reconciled to each other before making our offering tells us there is no way to give God wholeness of adoration and worship if the heart is mired down in grudges, hatred, indifference. Likewise in the Christian view, there is no way to get out of that swamp of hostility and indifference except through likeness to the Master, through the grace which makes us like him.

That there are examples of good, loving people who do not take part in the celebration of Jesus' self-giving death only confirms that God's grace is not limited by even the sacraments, that this self-giving is the all-inclusive pattern for human wholeness and that apart from the church and her worship human beings may still participate in the universal saving will of the Father.

Worship is for the glory of God and the transformation of believers, two purposes or ends that ideally coalesce. To the degree that we are enabled to serve our neighbor, to that degree God is worshiped.

A Tension to Tolerate

Not their love, but the impotence of their love keeps today's Christians from—burning us at the stake.   —FRIEDRICH NIETZSCHE

If I could just arrange for her happiness first, [Scobie] thought, and in the confusing night he forgot for the while what experience had taught him—that no human being can really understand another and no one can arrange another's happiness.   —GRAHAM GREENE

I hate people who are intolerant.   —LAURENCE PETER

Speaking of a wedding he was going to back home, a student in the dining room said to me: "I would have given my right arm to marry that girl!" Though he may not have realized it, his remark was extraordinarily appropriate to the liturgy of that weekend. The Gospel was Mark 9:38-48: "If your hand causes you to sin, cut it off . . . etc." His own turn of speech demonstrated that this vehement language of Scripture is not all that foreign to our way of speaking. We use similar exaggeration to express intense feeling.

The same Gospel selection suggests at least one other important point about reading Scripture. The point: one cannot just jump into the Bible, pull out a word or phrase, and say: This is it, this is Jesus' teaching, this is the simple, unequivocal truth. In the same reading, for instance, we hear Jesus saying: "He that is not against us is for us." But in Luke (11:23) and Matthew (12:30) we find: "He who is not with me is against me." A quite different claim. Similarly throughout Scripture, teaching about love is balanced with a justification of anger at times. Or, we are told to be mature but elsewhere to be childlike. We are assured that salvation is the work of God and elsewhere are told to work out our salvation in fear and trembling.

127

What all this says and what we see when we look seriously into Scripture is that the Bible is no simpleminded book. We can't do what the fellow in the well-known anecdote did. He flipped open the Bible for some immediate advice and put his finger down first on the text: "Judas went out and hanged himself." Looking for something more immediately helpful, he tried again, laid down his finger and found: "Go thou and do likewise."

The fact is that the divine procedure was to go through the whole messy business of speaking to us through the life of a man who was misunderstood, who suffered and was killed. That life and its teachings he meant to be a challenge to our minds and hearts. To us the Father says: "See what he did and was, what he said. What is your response?" God certainly could have emblazoned a message on some eternal billboard in the sky, some unambiguous and bald proposition rendering all our thinking, weighing, and faith irrelevant. But, no, he gave us a person who requires from us a thoughtful response, a free choice.

The text from Mark illustrates this in regard to an important issue in which we find some of the complexity and balance of Jesus' and Scripture's teaching. I would like to emphasize one example of that balance, an example that leaves us with serious responsibilities. When Jesus' followers in that text complain about an unauthorized man driving out devils, Jesus' answer is generously tolerant: "He that is not against us is for us." God will act, in other words, apart from twelve apostles, the Bible, a chosen people, sacraments, and Roman Catholics. More broadly, Jesus is telling us that we must be tolerant of those who are not in our club.

The other side of the coin appears in the "butchering" sections of the same reading: "If your foot is your undoing, cut it off. . . . If it is your eye, tear it out. . . ." To regard particular actions as so bad that we must take drastic measures means having some serious and intense convictions, some standards, some beliefs—at least and above all, where our own behavior is involved.

We are to combine the tolerance voiced in Christ's earlier remark with the intensity of belief enunciated in the "cut-it-off" section. The two are related in a way that even the dictionary definition concedes. There tolerance is defined as recognizing and respecting the views and practices of others even though not sharing them. Or as Teddy Roosevelt said: "We must learn to combine intensity of conviction with a broad toleration of difference of conviction."

Toleration and strong views go together. Convictions, beliefs, and persuasions are the condition for toleration. Someone has said it is easy to be tolerant when we do not care. But really, when we do not care, there is nothing to tolerate. We are actually not tolerating; we are merely letting everything wash over us indifferently, not distinguishing chocolate from garlic, crisp from mushy, Attila the Hun from Mother Teresa, right from wrong.

History and contemporary phenomena both illustrate that a strong sense of what is right or a conviction about some truth *can* lead to intolerance. That's part of the risk of being human and a great part of the sorry history of humanity. The New Testament calls us to dedication to truth while urging us to be tolerant of those who fail our standards or deny our beliefs. (While we tend to think of this problem in terms of what we tolerate, it is always in order to remind ourselves of how much others must tolerate in us. Also, many of us may need at times to be reminded to tolerate or forgive many things *in ourselves* that are due to our frailty and not easily overcome.) Obviously, there are limits. A society or an authority may have to say no very firmly and with sanctions to mass murder, intimidation, rape, torture, or some antisocial philosophy. And it should not be out of the realm of possibility for anyone of us to correct a friend or family member after carefully weighing the matter.

Without going further into an outline of a course in moral theology, it should be clear that tolerance is no simple matter. True tolerance presupposes a world in which we risk drawing the line for ourselves—that is where we are safest and can be most sure—and, indeed, at times, painful as it may be, for others. The element of risk involved when others are concerned should make us think twice about drawing the line for them and, when in doubt, to come down on the side of generosity.

All this, once again, simply says that neither Scripture nor life is immediately transparent and clear. Both ask a response rooted in reflection, discrimination, counsel, prayer, and prudence. The judicious practice of tolerance is most probable in the context of a well-rounded Christian life. The tension between tolerance and conviction is itself something we must learn to tolerate.

Mistakes about Mystics

> In the religious sphere, in particular, belief that formulas are true can never wholly take the place of personal experience. —WILLIAM JAMES

> People are generally better persuaded by the reasons which they have themselves discovered than by those which have come into the mind of others. —BLAISE PASCAL

> Yet, I repeat once more, the existence of mystical states absolutely overthrows the pretention of non-mystical states to be the sole and ultimate dictators of what we may believe. —WILLIAM JAMES

When is "Free and Easy" playing? the voice on the other end of the phone inquired. I was answering the phone in place of the local priest and someone apparently had a wrong number. (If I had been more alert I might have responded: "Sundays at 10 and 11:30." The parish was well known for a very informal liturgy that aroused active participation.) Later in the day I ran across an ad in the entertainment section of the newspaper about a group called "Free and Easy," who were playing at a local club. Appearing on the same program were "Merlin, Spangle, and the Mystics." That use of *mystics* is typical; for many, words like *mystic, mystical,* and *mysticism* have as much precision as *nice* does in popular usage.

Anything to any degree odd or unusual is an apt target for the term *mystical.* A newspaper article says that the governor of California "has probably unfairly been labeled a mystic." In other words, he is in the same class as an embezzler or some kind of social deviant. A poster bills a speaker as a mystic when all it means apparently is that the speaker does card tricks. A psychoanalyst speaking of people feeling disoriented or going in for meditation or other Oriental practices says they are "regressing into mysticism." A song says, "If California slides into the ocean, like the mystics and statistics say it will . . . ." There is endless justification for what my dictionary gives as the *third* meaning of mysticism: "vague, obscure, or confused thinking or belief."

To simplify a longer analysis it seems safe to say that mysticism conjures up for many these three notions: (1) it indicates something fuzzy, strange, or esoteric, something like magic, fortunetelling, seances, etc.; or (2) it suggests the various movements, often with Oriental connections, designed to give one serenity, success, or an increased efficiency at basketball, typing, or accounting; or (3) it means something like fleeing the world or being out of touch with hard reality.

Further observation would confirm that mysticism has a blurred if not dubious image. Fortunately, genuine authorities like Thomas Merton and Evelyn Underhill—and even my dictionary—still define mysticism as living, direct contact with God, an awareness of being in relation to God or a direct intuition of him. In the context of Christianity a personal pronoun like *him* is necessary because the experience uses the language of personal relationships and presumes a loving communion with a God capable of loving and receiving love.

Mysticism as direct contact with God, experience of his presence, is in the best Christian tradition exemplified in people like St. Augustine, St. John of the Cross, St. Teresa of Avila, the Quaker George Fox, and very possibly Dag Hammarskjold. In this tradition it has nothing essentially to do with things that "go bump in the night" or with moving objects at a distance. It may *incidentally* have something to do with trances, visions, etc., but these are not central and, in fact, the greatest mystics were embarrassed by such happenings or felt they witnessed more to human weakness than to anything necessarily divine.

More serious are the other misconceptions of mysticism as self-centered or aiming only at some new power or type of success or, finally, that of mysticism as a retreat from the world and its problems, an abandonment of one's neighbor and reality.

The idea that mysticism refers to some technique such as meditation or some similar exercise designed to bypass psychotherapy or solve emotional problems or, better yet, make one successful or relaxed— this idea has great currency today. A song by one Biff Rose a few years ago put it well: "I don't know why I'm not rich and famous; last month alone I logged four hundred hours of meditation." Similarly at the beginning of the film *Butch Cassidy and the Sundance Kid:* the latter is whipping an opponent in cards and the loser, itching for the film's first gun draw, asks to what the Kid attributes his success in cards. With a poker face he replies, "Prayer."

The prayer, meditation, and asceticism of genuine mystics are not for some obvious gain and profit. They are not even primarily for peace of soul; God more often seems to disturb than to pacify mystics. They do not pray or meditate in order to be able to see the progress in their spiritual biceps. For them prayer and meditation are to their relation to God what communication and conversation are to human relations: they are the stuff of it. They need no further justification, any more than human relations need further justification. If they are *for* anything, it is for an increase of love. A close relation to God in prayer is good whether or not it lowers one's blood pressure or gets one a promotion.

The attempt to achieve some special power or knowledge is the goal of magic or, with more reason, of various kinds of education or science but not of genuine mysticism. The latter seeks only to increase a union with God in love, a likeness to Christ. To attempt to use God, in effect, for health or efficiency is quite an inversion from the point of view of Scripture. Deepened personal union with God certainly should issue in better relations with others. Scripture and the mystics agree on the indivisibility of the love of God and of neighbor. Ultimately the test of genuine mystical life must always be the mystic's growth in unselfishness and genuine love for others. The life of the mystic is but an intensification of the life of an ordinary Christian and to be judged by the same criteria.

The charge that the life of a contemplative is a flight from the world and responsibilities is a bit more complex. In an extreme sense, anyone who is not out on the lines with the farm workers or with the South African mine workers is copping out—so one could argue. There is no simple test of when one is involved properly, since involvement can be of various kinds, suited to one's abilities and vocation. The possible types of involvement increase, too, as one admits the reality of such things as grace and recognizes the power of prayer, albeit little understood by the simply rational self.

The greatest practitioners of prayer do show the fruits of their union with God in heightened love and service of neighbor: in our own day Thomas Merton or Mother Teresa of Calcutta have shown this. While close to God in prayer, they do remember their zip code, how much detergent to put in the washer, and the sufferings of their neighbors. Some have been in the forefront of care of the sick, of helping the poor, of working for peace.

It remains true, nevertheless, that some are more famous for silence, solitude, and, in some cases, suffering. The believer should be able to see the possibility of value in these whether or not one is called to them. At a minimum we owe those who opt for prayerful union with God in solitude or withdrawal the same kind of tolerance we owe those who do other "useless" things like painting pictures, climbing Mount Everest, or playing the oboe. None of us can thoroughly and consistently expect to apply some naive standard of productivity and utility to the lives of others. Or if we attempt to do so, we do it only at the price of a frightening diminution of human life.

There is also the whole matter of the undoubtedly difficult and elusive truths that are part of the Christian faith, the communion of saints, for instance, or the truth enshrined in the vine and the branches. None of us knows simply and in detail how change of heart and changes in our world are brought about. Certainly our work and intelligence are essential, peace conferences are necessary, human ingenuity is indispensable, but is that all there is? The more "mystical" truths of Christianity and the lives of the mystics testify to more. They witness to other dimensions of God, above all to his transcendence: that he is not simply identifiable with the world and our activity or with our *perception* of his activity but capable of working in ways beyond our ken—in response to prayer, for instance.

Finally, most positively, all of us need something like what the mystics experience. Belief in and trust in God and Christ cannot simply be developed by reason and theology, essential as they are. Most of us need some experience (and the word is not simply synonymous with emotion), no matter how inexplicable or untransferable to others, which tells us it is worthwhile giving God worship and serving and loving both his difficult and his lovable people. The charismatic experience may provide this for some type of person. A satisfying and inspiring liturgy may do it for others. As other essays in this collection point out we cannot, of course, go out and pick up the experience but we can prepare and dispose ourselves for it.

Karl Rahner has written, "The Christian of the future will be a mystic or he will be nothing." That is, Christians will have experienced something of the reality of God—where or how makes little difference—or they will have nothing to support them in a more and more secularized society and world. Ultimately, even Christ's own invitation to us is in great part: Taste and see; try it; experience what I say.

"If religion cannot be equated with religious experiences, neither can it long survive their absence." Mysticism is not all of religion any more than is liturgy, church finance, or ethics, but it deserves more of our attention than it is usually given. In its widest sense mysticism as inclusive of religious experience on various levels, whether personal or communal, transitory or lasting, quiet or ecstatic, touches the reality of God, of meaning and purpose in our existence.

The Congenial Community, or—the Possible Parish

If you can find a church that is perfect, by all means, join it; but realize that when you do, it has ceased to be perfect.   —ANDREW GREELEY

(Writing of life in the church): To expect too much is to have a sentimental view of life and this is a softness that ends in bitterness. . . . I suppose it is like marriage, that when you get into it, you find it is the beginning, not the end, of the struggle to make love work. . . . The operation of the Church is entirely set up for the sinner; which creates much misunderstanding among the smug.   —FLANNERY O'CONNOR

You must believe in God, my child, whatever the clergymen say.
—BENJAMIN JOWETT to MARGOT ASQUITH

Some of the unchurched are satisfied that they have "met the Lord" in their private lives. That is enough for them, they say; they have found peace in him. Maybe, but with no church to shake up their joints and marrow from time to time (with sermons they don't want to hear, Scripture passages they would avoid, association with people outside their chosen circle), we may wonder whether they have found peace or simply shut their eyes to his reality.   —GEORGE MCCAULEY, S.J.

That the Church is of divine institution seems to me to be proved by the fact that no merely human institution could have survived a fortnight under such incompetent management.   —H. BELLOC

One shouldn't delegate the preaching of the Gospel entirely to others and then sit back and see how they do it.   —JURGEN MOLTMANN

When the thought first came of putting together such essays as these, I was talking with a friend, a fellow priest. Half-jokingly, somewhat ironically, we thought they might be entitled "And They're *Still* Cath-

135

olics" since we were discussing all the horrors, great and small, with which lay people have to put up from us priests. Horror is my somewhat dramatic term for everything from annoyance to outrage. After recounting respective lists of such, we could not but admire the faith and forgiving nature of the lay people who endure so much in us. (It is only right to note the somber truth that some—a good number possibly —have found these horrors more than they can take and have severed relations with the church.) We had in mind the trials, scandals, nuisances, insults, and injuries that come to members of the church primarily in the local parish setting or in dealing with us priests, though not this exclusively. Some of the actions of the church on the international level are often more disturbing than these local lapses. In general, of course, these problems may seem minimal when set against the background of the Inquisition or cases of ecclesiastical blessing of war or oppression. But sufficient for the day, the time, and the place are the horrors thereof.

Given the increasingly accepted pluralism of thought and practice in the church, there will be some disagreement about what constitutes a certified horror. One person's program may be another's pogrom. One person's celebration is often another's lamentation. But granted all that, there are still some acts and practices which would meet general recognition as offensive, undesirable, at least jolting.

To detail these would be an endless and sometimes comic, sometimes appalling, task but in order to be clear about what is meant here a few examples are necessary. No rating of these in terms of importance or reality is meant by their order. E.g., the multiple collections that characterize and clutter the Mass in so many Catholic churches. (At times one is tempted to make it a rule of thumb that it is not a bona fide Catholic church if there is not at least one collection; two or more assure that it is not only Catholic but also one, holy, and apostolic.) The authoritarianism (petty or otherwise) of church people at times as when, e.g., a parochial school regulates the *type of book satchel* students are to have. The betrayal of the spirit and purpose of the liturgy at important moments: a sermon on Easter Sunday which is, in effect, another sermon on Mary, pointing out—with no biblical evidence—that the first thing Jesus did on rising was to run to his mother. The obsession of hierarchy and individual priests, at times, with sexual morality and decency to the neglect of more central matters. An automatic and hurried celebration of the liturgy. Constant harping on one or a few subjects such as abortion or money or even some very petty preoccupation such as where people sit. Unprepared, rambling sermons. Dismissal of individual problems with stereotyped answers or paternalistic nostrums, etc. We could all make our lists. As critical priests—and, of course, ourselves presumably immune from complaints by a lay person regarding *our* manner of doing things!—we thought that Catholics often put up with a great deal just in the course of their weekly attendance at church. If we were in the layman's seat, what would we do? By the way, it is an irreplaceable experience and to be recommended to all priests that they attend Mass as part of a congregation at times.

To some the standard (and they would say "faith-filled") response to all this is: "We must accept that" and "the effects of the Mass, etc., are not dependent on the priest's personality, etc." With due regard to the type of faith represented by these statements, it must still be said that matters are not quite that simple.

It would help, difficult as it might be, to distinguish real from apparent scandals on the part of the clergy and representatives of the church, religious women and men, catechists, theologians, etc. Though part of the answer to all this is that we should all recognize that "we" are the church as well, in line with the limited scope of this essay, we will limit our remarks to the sort of problem that spokespersons and functionaries of the church raise for the lay person. Real or apparent scandals: how does one distinguish? Unwillingness of the local priest(s) to hear complaints or accept suggestions. An insensitive and daunting parish secretary or rectory housekeeper. The inability of church leaders, for instance, to offer any sort of spiritual leadership, but instead to merely repeat woodenly the content of make-work papers from the secretary of some Roman congregation. Putting the feelings and sentimental needs of a priest over the good of a parish. Are these apparent or real difficulties?

Some of the scandal to the laity of the church from the preaching or teaching of a priest or theologian is undoubtedly simply attributable to lack of information or a malformed conception of Christian teaching on the part of the lay person. If we think that every document originating in Vatican City—for example, the encyclical on marriage and birth control, *Humanae Vitae*—shares some sort of aura of infallibility, that is more our problem, often, than that of the author. Though it must be admitted that some of the authors, church authorities, and priests seem intent on making the umbrella of infallibility into a plastic bubble covering a multitude of statements. Similarly, to regard every public statement of a local pastor as indisputable is our error no matter how much a particular priest might be willing to accept this. If we are surprised that a minister of the church should be capable of anger or any other human feeling, we, of course, have an erroneous conception of what grace may do to human nature. Shock and scandal are not simply the result of insensitivity, bad morals, or stupidity on the part of priest or bishop or teacher but also the result of our being uninformed and, often, unwilling to take the necessary steps to be informed. Adult education about the faith should not be simply something that clergy and others interested have to trick intelligent adults into, but something we all sense as an obligation.

To go a little further afield for a moment. We should be aware of the temptation for all of us to weasel out of the implications of faith and commitment by piling up a collection of deterring shocks and offenses attributed to someone else's ill will rather than to our idleness or indifference. Our difficulties and doubts are often our evasions, our only partially admitted ways of avoiding commitment or the challenge to change.

Believing is much like love—they are, in fact, inseparable—and when we introduce another person into our lives in any serious way we open ourselves to demands, risks, and the need for some selflessness. And adult Christianity at the very least must involve a personal following of Jesus Christ. Presuming we recognize our responsibility in this matter and still find real obstacles to Christian life in the place where the church becomes real for us, in our parish situation, what do we do?

Since the parish church or its equivalent—that place where we meet with other Christians for the celebration of our faith and unity in Christ —is often the only place where many Christians come in contact with the organized church at all, that will be the focus of the rest of this essay. What do we do when life there, even if it is only on the average of an hour—but an important hour—a week, is anywhere from unsatisfying to intolerable? Our judgment about this is to some degree subjective but one of the matters we are more and more forced to understand is that, however relative the value of individual feelings, etc., they are nevertheless real and significant for the individual.

The Local Parish
Some Catholics with a loose or uninformed relation to the church may not even be aware that the church divides areas geographically and says that if one lives within the boundaries of North Elm and West 3rd Streets, one "belongs" to St. Harold's. Such ignorance can be blissful. Undoubtedly part of the rationale for the territorial parish dates from times when geographical convenience was a primary consideration. Possibly energy considerations will once again leave us no choice but to worship at a spot within walking distance of our homes. In that "no choice" I have

already betrayed some acceptance of the practice of going beyond the immediate territorial parish. Before we look at that option more closely, let us try to give the territorial parish its due.

Basic to the neighborhood parish seems to be a concept of the relative immobility of people; lives are generally lived in a limited area. If one lives in the Kenwood area one shops there, meets friends there, associates with neighbors there, interests oneself in improvements of the area, participates in recreational and social opportunities, etc. One belongs to the athletic and social groups formed in the area, etc. But is this really what happens? Do not people often live in one place and work and recreate in totally different places? Obviously, there are differences here between city-dwellers and those living in less densely populated, more remote areas—the latter may not have as many choices.

Some sort of physical structure for worship is part of the local parish. The traditional parish provides that those living within its boundaries help maintain whatever structures there are and, in a sense, tries to guarantee that support by declaring that one's address determines one's parish. Not only the church building but meeting places for instruction, even a full-blown school, and a place for social purposes all require and deserve support from those who will benefit from them. To imagine the community of Christians as something ethereally unconcerned with buildings, space, and an address would be to misconceive entirely the incarnational aspects of being a Christian. Even the Quaker founder, George Fox, who rejected church buildings, had to settle for meeting houses. As the Lord became a first-century Jew in Palestine, we too are Christians only in Dubuque, Dallas, or Delano, in the century of the great energy crunch and nuclear worry. Like the sacraments, a place set aside for worship pinpoints and focuses our relation to God. Moreover, if we are going to love and serve God's people and thus him, a particular place and specific group of people help assure that such service is real and responsible, not merely a one-shot variation from an otherwise self-centered life like the ten-minute visit of the movie star to the lepers' colony.

Regular participation in the life of the local parish should assure that one is exposed to a range of people not all of whom one would have voluntarily chosen as associates. Ideally this is so. In actuality a particular neighborhood may be so homogenized that one does not meet a wide variety of people. In rural and small-town areas, one is perhaps more likely to find oneself in a congregation consisting of the elderly, the young, business people, and workers: people I like and people I don't.

The parish as traditionally conceived and in the time and place of its inception may have guaranteed more of this mixture and catholicity than we can now be assured.

Some local parishes may still provide a natural and varied community, a place where one exercises some genuine commitment to others. (Needless to say, any "real" parish offers more of this than does the "electronic church," the TV evangelists.) But, as some of our passing qualifications have suggested, this may be minimal. Add to this the dissatisfaction (detailed earlier) people often experience with the life and practice of a particular parish and we have reason, I think, to give serious consideration to more mobility and to individual choice. To insist that the local parish—no matter how much it fails to fulfill all these needs and no matter how personally irritating an individual finds the manner of celebration and of parish life—is irreplaceable would be to put too much weight on objective, nearly magic matters, on institutions that are definitely outworn for many. If the manner in which the life of Christ is made present among us is a totally irrelevant consideration, then we could as well strip the church of *all* concern about music, art, mode and manner of preaching and teaching, and state baldly that being present in our local parish church once a week for a minimum of forty-five minutes is automatically conducive to salvation. Certainly we touch a delicate matter here. We recognize with St. Paul that the great message, the Gospel, is always being borne by earthly vessels. But are there not such things as cracked vessels, containers that cannot hold their contents?

The Chosen Parish
In actuality, people, with the help of the mobility we take for granted today, are choosing their parishes, forming communities based on other factors than geographical proximity. One innovative and lively parish in a large city reports that 80 percent of its worshipers come from outside the parish boundaries, some from twenty miles away. More ambitious observers might, of course, suggest earth- and people-moving measures for our cities, for our civilization, but I am concerned here to face the situation as it exists at present for many a thinking, concerned Christian.

Is the practice of "shopping" (to use the pejorative term) for a suitable parish consistent with the values we noticed in the local parish? Is the very project not simply a form of spiritual self-seeking? Does it neglect the God-given power of the church's worship in order to overemphasize my own satisfaction and feeling? Does it encourage personality cults among the clergy? Is it an implicit snobbishness? Is it in danger of identifying the power of the word with rhetoric and worldly panache, the power of the sacraments with their esthetic setting and emotional impact? Should those who are not content with their canonical parish be told they are poor Christians? Is it a matter of obedience being preferable to satisfying worship? Is the effort to find a congenial parish just a disguise enabling one to flee all concrete Christian responsibilities?

The situation for many is such that their involvement in the sacramental life of the church is going to be at a place of their choice or not at all. Though there may be no question of the church physically coercing people, we do exert moral coercion by some of the regulations about marriage, baptism, etc., which at their most wooden make life very difficult for those whose own conscience persuades them they must worship elsewhere than at their "parish" church. Possibly it is a matter of canon law catching up with the *de facto* situation of many people in a world different from that of centuries ago. Again, the problem may be compounded by the imperialistic interpretation or exercise of the law on the part of priest or bishop, itself an example of the kind of problem with which we began this discussion. The only thing accomplished by intransigence and resistance to the mobility of people today is a furtherance of alienation from Christianity. The actual pluralism in the Catholic church today, a pluralism which deserves more respect and acceptance than we have thus far given it, means that people can find a church which continues to have Benediction or one that sponsors a group for divorced Catholics. *Vive la difference!* A little more of that spirit might have softened some of the bitterness of the Reformation and also of the aftermath of Vatican II.

In choosing a parish the major pitfalls to be avoided seem to be elitism and escapism. The first is that snobbish seeking of a group of like-minded people, like-minded to the extent that ultimately they offer no stimulation to us, but only a confirmation of our status quo, no matter how much in need of amendment. The frictionless type of existence that would be sought in associating at worship with only "our kind of people" is sterile and historically has led to heights or depths of self-satisfaction and exclusivism inconsistent with the Gospel. To hear or to encounter only what we have predetermined to be worth hearing or encountering is the beginning of a kind of spiritual death. And, of course, it is ultimately unrealistic: such seeming congeniality and agreement cannot be real or last for long. And, when resented, they become the occasion for bitterness and disillusionment.

Escapism refers to the implicit desire to avoid the full range of human reality, not to have to face certain ineluctable facets of human existence. Faithfulness to the cycles of Scripture texts now provided for in our liturgy is itself meant to guarantee us some exposure to parts of the word of God that, of ourselves, we might not heed. A variety of people and a variety of texts can conduce to expanding our minds and hearts. Escapism means also the intention, in choosing one's parish or, further, never settling on *one* at all, of remaining free of any commitments to people, projects, and programs which would implement the Gospel. The definition of such escapism is its own condemnation.

All of this has been stating that communities are not simply given to us but also made by us. When individual factors in our geographical community are such that only death, revolution, or some untoward divine intervention are going to remedy them—at least for us—then we need to seek and find a community that will nourish us and to which we can contribute also. The idea is not all that exceptional in the church. Religious communities of men and women have illustrated it for centuries. If to find and join a congenial community were *ipso facto* an act of disobedience, an assertion of mere self-will, and a rejection of the human condition, the church should never have approved these thousands of communities throughout the ages which have meant so much to its life.

If looking for and finding a congenial community—as the alternative to the frustration induced by the little or great horrors we discussed earlier—is to be a positive step, if it is to be our part in a creative work ("making community"), it will mean more than just passive attendance. It will require involvement, the gift of self to and work for that particular community of Christians and for those whom it hopes to touch. It will demand our support of the community in all ways including financial. We will do our part to forward the good things that have drawn us to it. With good fortune, this community will be of the sort where one may speak frankly and directly of problems or aspirations and be assured of a hearing. Often that in itself helps assuage our discontent with aspects of a parish or community program. These latter points, once again, remind us that the scandals and obstacles presented to belief by "the church" are usually partly of our own making: we all so easily serve in some way or other as more of a wall than a bridge for those drawn to life in Christ.

It is the Lord Jesus Christ whom John's Gospel proclaims as the Way, the Truth, and the Life—not the Bible, tradition, or the church. They and we must point to the Lord, to God. The Bible attests to him, tradition and the church are there to transmit his life and Spirit. But they remain only monuments and museums for relics of the Savior unless, by hope and confidence in him and love and service for his world, we and *our* church appear as witnesses to him. The church and all its functions and ministers and practices need to point beyond themselves to the Way, the Truth, and the Life. Otherwise they are the obstacles of which we have been treating and serve rather to hide than reveal the God of love. In a manner modeled after Christ himself the church, its members and ministers, are meant to give a face, a voice, and hands to the Way, the Truth, and the Life. What we demand rightly of the rest of the church and its ministers we must be always prepared to demand of ourselves, too, whatever our position in the church. Really there is no *they* (ministers, bishops, pope) and *we* in the church. All of us are the church and it is limited as a life-giving and saving instrument of God to the degree that we are not transparent but opaque, not a way but a cul-de-sac, not a bridge but a wall.

With the Wrong Crowd

The world is divided into those who want to become someone and those who want to accomplish something. . . . there is less competition in the second category. —JEAN MONNET

I do not have to believe in Christ in order to work for a better world. But if I believe in Christ, then I must work for a better world. —HANS KÜNG

For a Christian there is no choice between personal sanctification and social and political involvement. —JEAN JADOT

What if Jesus after rising from the dead had decided to avoid his old crowd and his old enemies and settle down in some quiet spot in Lapland or Manitoba or Syria? D. H. Lawrence, a twentieth-century novelist, did invent such a postresurrection life for Jesus in a story he wrote. In it Jesus rises and, without returning to his Father or to his friends, tells the latter by his actions to unload their troubles on someone else. He's going to, as we say, "live his own life."

For those at all familiar with the Gospels and Christian belief that, of course, is poor theology and poor history, whether or not it's good literature. The real story of Jesus is one of unstinting involvement. Even his postresurrection appearances are concerned with his followers and their future. And it was so from the beginning of his public life. One of the first events covered in the Gospels is the baptism of Jesus by John the Baptist, in Matthew and Mark. Baptism at its most basic is an acted-out prayer admitting the need for forgiveness and asking that evil be washed away, as grime and sweat are washed away by bathing.

By undergoing this rite at John's hands Jesus showed clearly how total was his commitment to human life. He placed himself not only squarely in our world but on the side of sinners. Apparently the first Christians, very much impressed with the sinlessness of the Son of God,

144

at some stage found this identification with the guilty almost too much to accept. They seemed to have been inclined to minimize it. In Luke's Gospel (3:21), for instance, the baptism of Jesus is mentioned almost incidentally: "But when Jesus also had been baptized and was praying...." In John's Gospel there is reference to John baptizing (chapters 3 and 4) but no mention that Jesus was ever baptized. Later on Christians were able to rejoice in the baptism of the Lord as an undeniable sign of how genuinely Jesus shared their life.

The whole matter of God becoming man in Jesus is, of course, the model of voluntary and generous involvement, going out of one's way to be involved. What God does in the human life of Jesus is a much-magnified version of what happens when we forego our own comfort, convenience, and schedule to help others. We let a long-awaited ski trip give place to sleepless nights and worry as we stay close to a suddenly sick member of the family or a friend. We pass up some party with our hale and hearty friends to talk to a depressed—and maybe even depressing—friend. What we are talking about is not some token kind of involvement—the kind of slumming that takes place when a top-level executive spends fifteen minutes in the boiler room or a celebrity flies to Cambodia for a well-televised day in the jungle with the refugees—but a commitment to sharing pain and difficulty.

In the case of Jesus this involvement went so far that his opponents complained about his lack of discrimination, blamed him for hanging around with the wrong crowd. (In the end he hangs on the cross between two thieves.) In responding to his critics Jesus essentially blamed it all on poor family background, the bad example of his Father, Yahweh, whose initiatives were recorded in their history. And he told some parables. One spoke of the Father as being more concerned about the one lost sheep than the ninety-nine who were safe; another compared him to a woman who turned the house upside down to find some lost money. Similarly, he said, God is concerned to find and save the lost, the abandoned, the weak, and the despised.

To the great act of God's involving himself in our life we respond best by echoing that involvement in our concern for the hurting, the hungry, the lonely, the despairing, the withdrawn, the unwanted, the inconsequential. One hopes that the question which arises for most of us is not *why* should I do this, or *should* I do this, but rather *how much* should or can I do.

And the involvement must begin with specific people and situations, *now*. But where? With whom? We can't be everywhere and do everything for everyone from Calcutta to Colombia, with stops at Council

Bluffs. But we can begin with those who have a natural claim on us: families, dependents, our immediate neighbors, the people we regularly meet in the course of daily life. As we give them time and attention we find it more and more difficult to restrict the number of claimants.

But at least to some of these people we must make some response. We cannot forever excuse ourselves from all involvement on the plea of preparing for a career or advancing our position no matter how humanitarian we plan and intend that to be. Self-development, keeping up on one's field, etc., all have legitimate claims on us but not rights that suspend our responsibilities as members of and followers of Christ, the healer and comforter.

How much involvement remains undeniably the practical problem, the question. And no one can answer it for anyone else. Presuming we understand that our present, our future, and our satisfaction are not the final norms for what we do with our life and time, positively the following of Christ means engagement with and for others. If we do not begin now, we will always be able to find excuses for not doing anything later on. That neglected person we've met and talked with, a worried friend, a hurting neighbor who is afraid to complain, the family member who tries not to disturb us with some problem back home—some of these must benefit from our faith, hope, ability, kindness, attention, our special gifts of character and personality.

Paradoxically, answering the needs of others is one of the surest ways of bringing out and developing our own best gifts. No one knows what capacities for sympathy he or she has till some grief-stricken person calls on those powers; no one knows how understanding he or she can be till some confused person pours a jumble of questions into the listening ear. A great part of our growth consists in allowing the needs of others, the demands of our milieu, to draw us out of ourselves into the problems of others and thereby into an expanded vision of life, into that self-development that so often concerns us.

Nevertheless, giving self and time to those we may not be spontaneously attracted to, forgetting ourselves in their needs—all this is difficult. We are easily tempted to give it up at times, to withdraw into ourselves or to the comfort of a few old friends. Either because we have been working hard at it or because we are not spiritually up to the demands, the actual commitment can be wearing. For that reason, our involvement needs to be fueled by close contact with the power and grace of Christ. Like the Christ depicted in Luke's Gospel we need prayer, retreat from involvement, in order to maintain our strength, to insure the persistence and purity of our motivation.

The rhythm of engagement and withdrawal is ultimately a matter to be determined by the individual in terms of the level of his or her spiritual life, in terms of what one knows he or she can ask of self and give without appearing the martyr. Only you and I can finally make the decisions which balance personal development, family needs, and responsibilities to our world in a way that is possible and practicable here and now in our lives. The Christian needs here as in so many other areas to be willing to develop and trust her own conscience, to take his own conscience seriously, to realize that it, like everything else in our life in Christ, is in process of growth, never finished, never mathematically clear.

To reflect the initiative of the Father and the Son by seeking out and helping the lost and undesirable, the needy and suffering, remains an inexhaustible and at times exhausting ideal. It also remains an unavoidable consequence of the following of Christ. "Lord, may I not seek so much to be consoled as to console, to be loved as to love, to be understood as to understand."

The Fantastic and the Familiar

Wisdom is ofttimes nearer when we stoop
Than when we soar. —WORDSWORTH

Religion at its best is a response to the deepest implications of our common
life, not something dependent on the extraordinary and the unusual. It
is rooted in appreciation of the meaning that lies all around us if we would
only listen and look. —*Interpreter's Bible*

I asked for all things that I might enjoy life,
   I was given life, that I might enjoy all things.
I got nothing that I asked for, but everything I had hoped for,
   My unspoken prayers were answered. —RABINDRANATH TAGORE

The Way is near, but men seek it afar. It is in easy things, but men seek
for it in difficult things. —MENCIUS

Sitting quietly, doing nothing,
Spring comes, and the grass grows by itself. —ZENRIN KUSHU

The increasing speed of modern life has done away with the meager leisure
we once had. Our ways of enjoying ourselves are hardly less irritating
and nervewracking than the pressure of our work. ("As much as possible,
as fast as possible" is the motto. . . .) I would simply recall: Moderate enjoyment is double enjoyment; Do not overlook the little joys.
—HERMANN HESSE

The "Fantastic and the Familiar" was finally chosen for this essay's
title over "The Striking and the Standard," "The Conspicuous and the
Conventional," "The Notable and the Normal," "The Exceptional and
the Expected."

In many ways the standard or the expected is more of a problem for
us than the unusual. A song points out that some days are like "diamonds."

But too many, of course, seem to be stones: dull, tedious, repetitive, meaningless. Things are really at their nadir when we merely or barely live or, rather, hang on five or six days a week or even months at a time in expectation of something out of the ordinary like downhill skiing, wine tasting in California, getting out of our job, or moving.

The familiar is just that—so familiar, so close, so taken for granted that it's often hard to see its goodness, appreciate its meaning, preserve its freshness. But I think that the fantastic—I'm using the term to cover all that is unusual, exceptional, magnificent, ecstatic, great and new, beautiful, or generous—exists in a real sense for the sake of the familiar, to point to the hidden possibilities and beauty of the everyday. As the Zen people seem to believe, we may need some shock to open up the ordinary to us. The unusual, the strange, the surprising, the breathtaking exceptions to routine are supposed to do that, I believe.

We can, of course, accept the ordinary unthinkingly and push away any questions about it as bizarre or excessive: "Don't you have anything better to do?" Or we are tempted to think of it solely in pessimistic ways. We ask *why* Monday, Tuesday, Wednesday, etc., breakfast, work, lunch, dinner, TV, sleep, breakfast, work, lunch, work, etc. Instead of marveling that Tuesday follows Monday, we moan: It's Sunday already or July's half over. We feel "sentenced to reality" (Peter Handke) rather than blessed with the gift of something fresh and incredible.

Though we think of the familiar as the opposite of the fantastic or the mysterious, on closer look the familiar is probably more mysterious. What is fantastic is not that someone has seen strange lights in the sky or heard unusual noises in a vacant house or seen a family member carried off by a troop of mosquitoes. What is mysterious is that people can be so thoughtful; that we smile to greet others; how people fall in love; that the smell of home is so welcome after a trip; that beauty sometimes takes our breath away; that good bread and drink can comfort us so much. It seems to me there is more mystery in the way of human attraction or the way the weather or music affect us than there is in fifty *Exorcist* films or in pictures of Saturn's rings.

The really fantastic things are simply marvelous or superabundant versions of something we have to some degree in ordinary life here and now. The wild artists and musicians from Mozart to Jim Morrison, a Van Gogh who cuts off an ear, the sculptor who makes stone breathe, the extraordinarily selfless people we call saints who make us question our cautious lives, the exhilarating spectacle of some great dancer or athlete—these seemingly exceptional people and creations point up what is available to us in ordinary life and ordinary people, at least potentially. The artists, musicians, saints, geniuses, and magnetic figures may be the peaks of the human terrain but they're of the same clay and composition as the slopes and valleys. They underline our capacity for gentleness, strength, boldness, generosity, self-giving, beauty, energetic action, care.

Specifically, in our religion, too, the strange things—the unusual, as, for example, the fuss about water and wine and bread accompanied by songs, gestures, and strange clothes (the Mass)—are meant to spotlight the significance of something so basic as eating and living together. The ritual, the liturgy, something set apart from ordinary life, exists for the sake of the ordinary, to open up the daily, to disclose its real meaning. Worship, James T. Burtchaell says, is an interlude in the actual business of salvation. We pause and celebrate those otherwise odd rites in order to be able to see the purpose and eternal worth of all the other things we do: our work, our recreation, the people in our lives, and our living with them. As the celebrant raises the symbols of ordinary life, bread and wine, he repeats the words of Jesus: "This is my body; this is my blood." Yes, this is where the Lord is: in the ordinary elements and people of daily life. Communion together reminds us that love is the indispensable seasoning in any genuine meal—that lasagne without love is lacking! Celebrating this ritualized meal with a token amount of wine and bread should help us recognize that the Lord is present whenever we eat and drink with others. Like the disciples in the Gospels, our eyes should be opened to recognize him at breakfast, banquet, or brunch.

Sunday, we might say, is for the sake of Monday through Saturday. The seven moments we call the sacraments exist for the sake of all the other moments of the year, reminding us that they are all contagious with grace. While marriage, for instance, celebrates an exclusive-appearing love of two people for each other, it also highlights the love and concern that should ideally enter into all our relationships, the extension of that love to all people.

By now, I'm sure what I've been saying is in need of defense against the charge of romanticizing. And certainly none of our experience of beauty, love, joy, and excitement in religion or any great human achievement guarantees that we carry over the lessons into the less extraordinary moments. "Some days are diamonds; some are stones." We don't easily make them all diamonds; some we continue to take for granite. Any real carry-over from the fantastic to the familiar requires an effort to make meals, for instance, a celebration of shared concern and love, to see the talent and goodness in those we are so used to. And the sacrament of marriage doesn't, obviously, do away with the need to work at that love.

Again, our celebration together on Sundays, it can't be too strongly stressed, does its work only with some effort to see the fantastic as related to the familiar. To concentrate on the Eucharist as some magical means for plunking the Lord down in our midst for a few golden moments while neglecting its function of relating us to each other would be seriously off target. We must come away from the Lord's Supper determined to genuflect (at least figuratively) before the mystery of ordinary life, the mystery of the people in our "hamburger-helper" kind of life.

This would be all too rosy a view if we neglected to see the cross in ordinary life and in our Eucharist. The association of the Eucharist with the cross—as often as you do this you show the death of the Lord—our calling it a memorial not only of the Last Supper but of the suffering and death of Jesus tells us how closely bound in human life are joy and community, suffering and growth. Again to go back to the fantastic and the familiar, the cross and crucifixion are dramatic and extreme forms of suffering but basically intensified forms of what the man or woman on the hospital bed endures or what the lonely elderly endure, of what we undergo in painful relationships and unpleasant work. Routine, worry, stress, illness, disputes, and arguments—all can be types of pain that come as unasked-for bonuses when we live and love the reality of ordinary life.

Some of the more notorious examples of the fantastic and exceptional—some great musicians, artists, maybe even some of the mystics—seem to be examples of escapism at times. Some of them streak across our skies like falling stars. Even the insane-appearing quest of some of them for continual ecstasy and excitement, of some unearthly ideal, testifies at least to a belief that every moment of life *should* be transfigured, should be better than it is. Even when these seekers of the unusual and exceptional fail to appreciate the necessity for drudgery and pain, they at least point to the ideal we're talking about: of seeing and creating beauty, joy, daring, excitement, a certain spaciousness, and a freedom in more of the moments and situations of daily life. By their revolt against what *is,* they herald what *should* be. More reprehensible really are the paperback prophets (and profiteers) of perpetual joy who write as if living every moment at full throttle in some ecstatic state were a real possibility for anyone with the price of the paperback.

A feast, of course, is only a feast if there are some days of peanut butter sandwiches or boiled cabbage. In that sense we must appreciate more the quietness and uneventfulness, the simplicity, even the routine of much ordinary life. A Zen saying puts it: "How marvelous, how miraculous; I draw water, I gather fuel." How wonderful: I have a coffee break, I pick up the kids at school, I meet David or Brenda on the street. Much of daily life, while slow and apparently unexceptional, is unavoidably so and not evil. But some of it is evil, not just sober and plain but dehumanizing, not just routine but destructive.

The Lord who taught us by his word and example that the way to glory goes through suffering and death thereby told us that there are demands to be made on life and self and the world. For the Christian it is never solely a matter of loving and accepting all that is *as it is*. Jesus' suffering and death were consequences of his resistance to life and his criticism of what was. He condemned injustice, hypocrisy, falsehood, self-seeking. Seeing the beauty and glory hidden in the ordinary cannot be equated with uncritical acceptance of it. Like those who have sought to exalt life by living in a dream world of stimulants and stimulation, we too should be dissatisfied with life. But instead of escaping into a never-never world, a world of illusion, we are called to draw on the power of the risen Christ in us to work for the transformation of *this* world.

Ultimately it comes down again to one of those personal decisions about how we will live, how each of us will respond on the basis of our experience, self-knowledge, and the call of God's grace. We must each work out a *possible* balance of what is acceptable in the familiar and what we see as demanding change and work. Each of us in his or her own circumstances must evaluate what *is* over against what might be or *should be*.

The fantastic examples in science and art, in medicine and engineering, in any human achievement, and the examples of courage, selflessness, and generosity in the saints all tell us what is already present in human life and what could be. George Bernanos wrote: "Grace is everywhere." The brilliant examples we see picture the transformation of life and our world achievable by God's gifts in all of us and by the power of the risen Lord's life in us. In appreciating the ordinary and the familiar, we see some of the glory, the fantastic, that shines in our world. Through improving the ordinary, seeing its limitations and working to better it, we help more of the familiar to become fantastic.

Acknowledgments

Grateful acknowledgment is made to the following for permission to reprint portions of copyrighted material:

Extracts from *Foundations of Christian Faith* by Karl Rahner. English translation copyright © 1978 by The Seabury Press. Used by permission of The Crossroad Publishing Company.

Extract from *God in the Dock* reprinted by permission of Curtis Brown, Ltd., London, on behalf of the Trustees of the Estate of C. S. Lewis.

Extract from *Love Within Limits* by Lewis Smedes. Used by permission of William B. Eerdmans Publishing Company, Grand Rapids, Michigan. Copyright © 1978.

Extracts from *The Habit of Being, The Violent Bear It Away,* and *Wise Blood* in *Three by Flannery O'Connor,* ed. Sally Fitzgerald. Used by permission of Farrar, Straus & Giroux, Inc.

Extracts from *My Belief* by Herman Hesse. Used by permission of Farrar, Straus & Giroux, Inc.

Extracts from *Getting Even* by Woody Allen. Copyright © 1972 by Random House, Inc. Used by permission.

CHURCH GROWTH

AND THE POWER OF

EVANGELISM

Ideas That Work

Howard Hanchey

COWLEY PUBLICATIONS
Cambridge, Massachusetts

Published in the United States of America by Cowley Publications, a division of the Society of St. John the Evangelist. No portion of this book may be reproduced, stored in or introduced into a retrieval system, or transmitted, in any form or by any means—including photocopying—without the prior written permission of Cowley Publications, except in the case of brief quotations embodied in critical articles and reviews.

International Standard Book Number: 1-56101-008-1 cloth
1-56101-017-0 paper
Library of Congress Number: 90-43921

Library of Congress Cataloging-in-Publication Data
Hanchey, Howard.
    Church growth and the power of evangelism : ideas that work / Howard Hanchey.
    p. cm.
    Includes bibliographical references.
    ISBN 1-56101-008-1 (alk. paper) — ISBN 1-56101-017-0 (pbk. : alk. paper)
    1. Church growth—United States. 2. Christian life—Anglican authors. 3. Christian education of adults. 4. Evangelistic work—United States. 5. Episcopal Church—Membership. 6. Anglican Communion—United States—Membership. I. Title.
BR526.H26 1990
254'.5—dc20   90-43921

This book is printed on acid-free paper and was produced in the United States of America.

Cowley Publications
980 Memorial Drive
Cambridge, Massachusetts 02138

To
David Shepherd Rose
and
T. Hudnall Harvey
both extraordinary priests
and teachers.